Sanctity Without Starch

A Layperson's Guide to a Wesleyan Theology of Grace

by

Robert G. Tuttle, Jr.

First Fruits Press
Wilmore, Kentucky
c2015

Sanctity without starch: a layperson's guide to a Wesleyan theology of grace.
By Robert G. Tuttle, Jr.

First Fruits Press, ©2016
Previously published by Bristol Books, 1992.

ISBN: 9781621714668 (print), 9781621714675 (digital)

Digital version at http://place.asburyseminary.edu/firstfruitsheritagematerial/119/

Tuttle, Robert G., 1941-
    Sanctity without starch : a layperson's guide to a Wesleyan theology of grace /
Robert G. Tuttle, Jr.
    203 pages : illustrations ; 21 cm.
    Wilmore, Kentucky : First Fruits Press, ©2016.
Reprint. Previously published: Lexington, KY : Bristol Books, 1992.
ISBN - 13: 9781621714668 (pbk.)
    1. Grace, (Theology) 2. Sanctification. 3. Holiness. 4. Christian life--Methodist
authors. I. Title.
BT761.2.T87 2016   234

Cover design by Jon Ramsay

asburyseminary.edu
800.2ASBURY
204 North Lexington Avenue
Wilmore, Kentucky 40390

First Fruits
THE ACADEMIC OPEN PRESS OF ASBURY SEMINARY

First Fruits Press
The Academic Open Press of Asbury Theological Seminary
204 N. Lexington Ave., Wilmore, KY 40390
859-858-2236
first.fruits@asburyseminary.edu
asbury.to/firstfruits

Sanctity Without Starch

To All Our Children:
Sarajane, Bill, Marilee, Eric, and Elizabeth

Sanctity Without Starch

A Layperson's Guide to a Wesleyan Theology of Grace

Robert G. Tuttle, Jr.

3

CONTENTS

ACKNOWLEDGEMENTS

Appreciation must be expressed to staff and students at Garrett-Evangelical Theological Seminary. First, thank you to Steve Sandage who (while walking together in a garden in Beijing, China) gave me an insight which sparked a need to complete a manuscript long in the making. I had been preaching on the connection between the power of grace/Holy Spirit and overcoming sin in persons and systems for five or six years (and with much fruit), but had managed to commit only five or six chapters to paper. After Steve's reminder of the importance of this connection and his challenge to pursue the project I returned to my computer and saw a manuscript move to completion in less than two months. Steve then critiqued the full manuscript.

Also thank you to Steve Rankin as well as the editorial staff at Bristol House, Ltd., who read the manuscript and made several valuable suggestions.

As with most of my written work here at Garrett-Evangelical Theological Seminary, I am deeply indebted to Helen Hauldren who types and organizes mounds of words and material without complaint. God keep her healthy. I am in deep trouble without her.

INTRODUCTION

Recently I met a young landscape architect who works for a large West Coast firm. After some small talk he asked me what I did for a living.

"I'm a minister," I replied.

He responded immediately that he was an atheist.

Somewhat intrigued, I asked, "How does a man who gets to work with nature's beauty get to be an atheist?"

"Just lucky, I guess," he boasted; "and why would anyone want to be a minister?"

While thinking to myself, *God, this man is going to be tough,* I continued, "Let me ask you another question. If you could know for certain that there really is a God who loves and cares for you and who makes a power available to sustain you in your life, would you be interested?"

"You bet," he stated with apparent conviction.

Looking at him rather intently, I simply added, "That's why I'm a minister. I want to help people just like you come to know that there really is a God who loves and cares for you and who makes a power available to sustain you in your life."

Somewhat to my surprise — God help my unbelief — he said, "Tell me more." Since we were seatmates on a long transcontinental flight that's precisely what I did. The turnaround had taken less than 60 seconds. Now, rather than working against me, he was for me. He actually encouraged me to explain to him the source of this God-given power.

As you might imagine my young architect friend envisioned himself as a "free-thinker," a bit of a maverick with an IQ matched only by his RQ (rebellion quotient). Yet, he was caught by the phrase, "a God who loves and cares and makes a power available to sustain you in your life." Although young, athletic and financially secure, he sensed a need for help, but God and religion had long been discarded under the guise of an old legalism that drove its adherents into fits of temporary submission (not unlike John Wesley's "transient fits of repentance").

His attempts to compensate involved several of the popular "self-help" philosophies which he soon found equally frustrating. He wanted this power. Although he did not know it yet, he wanted grace, and that is what I told him about.

The rest of us may not be atheists, but isn't that what we want as well? So, that is what I want to describe to you here — a simple Wesleyan plan of salvation (understanding of course, that the term "salvation," for Wesley, had implications long before and far beyond any single experience of Christian conversion). In other words, how does God's grace work in our lives, "soup to nuts?" How does the Holy Spirit work in our lives, "cradle to grave?"

So, our task is necessarily theological. Not to worry. The Scottish theologian Tom Torrence has said that "theology is merely the mind worshiping God." I like that. It smacks of simplicity. During the 60's the expression went, "If you want to impress them, confuse them. They will say, 'That's so deep! Heady stuff.'" We confused them all right. Much of our teaching came from the head and went to the head, but not much further. Many theologians sounded more like philosophers, others agnostics, and a few like atheists. We seemed to lose touch with the people and they lost touch with the church (in droves), at least with much of the so-called mainline churches.

Why not speak about theology that is deep because it makes us deep? John Wesley wrote: "My soul is sick of sublime divinity. Let me think and speak as a little child! Let my religion be plain, artless, simple!"[1] Why not write a book that teaches good theology in such a way as to catch the imagination while stirring the mind and spirit? Why not sanctity without starch?

Furthermore, why not a book that is concerned with a theology of Christian growth and development that is also a tool for evangelism as well? Historically evangelists have all too often not shown

theology that leads to transformation

much interest in theology, and theologians have not shown much interest in evangelism. Unashamedly, the intent here, although rarely mentioning the word "evangelism" (John Wesley set a pretty good precedent for that; I do not recall his ever using the term, he simply did it), is to lead you — at whatever level of faith and commitment — into a closer relationship with the living God who loves and cares for you.

Although no strategy for church growth will be developed, no how's and why's as to the principles of sharing the faith will be expounded, evangelism as well as Christain growth and development should be served. The purpose here is to describe the faith itself in such a way that insight will dawn, love will grow and understanding will appear as clear as the day.

As God's creation, we need to know that Christianity makes sense. My architect friend would not check his brain at the door of any church. He had a right to know that there are good reasons for believing in a God-given power. Too often we have seen bad theology deliver people into needless bondage, whereas good theology releases the captive. Good theology empowers us to overcome those things that would attempt to swallow us without stumbling from one ditch to another.

Someone has said, "If it didn't sound like good news, you haven't heard the gospel yet." That's the point. The gospel not only makes sense, it is good news. That's not to say that the gospel discards the Law — certainly not, the Law contains God's basic principles (epitomized by the Ten Commandments) for establishing right from wrong — *but neither is it grunt and groan*, a lifeless attempt to fulfill an imposible standard.

The gospel is life itself, abundant life. It is power, Holy Spirit power for fulfilling the Law, available by virture of one's faith in Jesus Christ, and no theology better describes that kind of good news than the theology of John Wesley. A healthy understanding of that theology could well change your life and keep it changed. The problem is how best to discuss some of the theological complexities involved without bogging down in terminology. Let me make an initial attempt for just a paragraph or two before moving on to the overall plan of the book itself.

A part of Wesley's genius lay in his ability to create balance between theological perspectives normally at odds with each other.

His bringing together the biblical teachings on law and grace is a classic example and best describes his overall approach to the Scripture way of salvation.

Not too long ago I was introduced to a young Muslim. After visiting for some time and getting acquainted, I remember asking him to describe to me the Islamic Law. He did so at some length and with real appreciation, but with considerable frustration at his inability to measure up. Then I asked if he really wanted to obey that Law.

His reply? "With all my heart. I've been trying to obey that Law for nearly 30 years."

At that point I simply said, "Sit down, I'm going to tell you a story." The story I told him? The story of Jesus Christ. The story of grace and the power of the Holy Spirit available through faith in him for fulfilling that Law.

His response? "What you are saying is that the only way for me to fulfill the Islamic Law is to become a Christian."

He got the point. Apart from grace, Law, *any* law, is a "law of sin and death." That point is so important that we will return to it time and again.

The gospel has been aptly described as good news/bad news/ good news. The first good news is that we are created in the image of God. The bad news is that we lose that image. The final good news is that God is in Christ reconciling the world, restoring us to our own created image, our original righteousness.

The problem with some is that they begin with the bad news. There is no original good news so there is nothing to which we might be restored, no original righteousness. Justification seems an end in itself with little impetus for sanctification to follow, a self-centered consumer Christianity which thinks only of itself.

The problem with others is that there is no bad news, only good news/good news and, since (according to these) we have *not* lost our ability to obey God out of our own human resources, there is no need for the reconciling work of God in Jesus Christ. Sanctification replaces justification in the plan of salvation, an other-centered works-righteousness Christianity which denies the needed power to pull it off.

Before we get too bogged down with terminology, however, let me introduce most of the crucial terms visually, in the form of a chart. Then, as we anticipate the chapters to follow, I will provide a key for that chart that can easily be used for reference throughout.

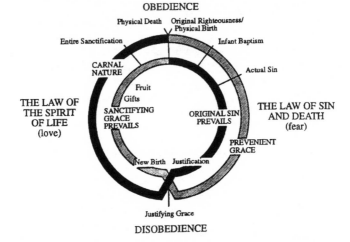

The circle itself represents one full life cycle. Notice the contrast from top to bottom. The top depicts obedience; the bottom depicts disobedience. From the top of the circle note the point of *original righteousness* accompanied by *physical birth*.

Original righteousness is the image of God that was resident in Adam and Eve before the fall. It is a propensity to do what was right and resist what was wrong whereby immortality was at hand and fellowship with God was immanent (or near at hand) and personal.

Physical birth itself might seem self-evident, but it is important to remember that life and human susceptibility, at least from a biblical point of view, begin at the moment of conception.

Then moving clockwise, note the darkly shaded area denoting the effects of *original sin* and the lighter shaded area denoting the effects of *prevenient grace* which seek to counter the effects of original sin.

Original sin is a propensity to sin that resulted from the disobedience of Adam and Eve whereby they lost their propensity for righteousness, immortality at hand and the close personal fellowship with God. This became part of the human condition inherited by all subsequent generations.

Prevenient grace is the Holy Spirit at work in everyone between conception and conversion. The Holy Spirit woos or *prevents* us from moving so far toward disobedience, that when we finally understand the claims of the gospel upon our lives, we are guaranteed the freedom to say yes.

Now, back at the chart note that prior to conversion, although *infant baptism* may accelerate the effects of prevenient grace, original sin nonetheless prevails, leading inevitably (with the exception of Jesus Christ, who alone was sinless) to *actual sin.*

Infant baptism is that sacrament in which the infant children of Christian parents are baptized (within a community of believers one would hope) so that the effects of prevenient grace are accelerated and the devastation of actual sin diminished.

Actual sin is our own personal sin that is committed upon the age of accountability (when we consciously understand the difference between right and wrong), a willful disobedience. It is important to remember John Wesley believed that one is not condemned for original sin alone but for original sin plus actual sin.

Now note at the bottom of the chart's circle, *justifying grace* reverses the process back toward obedience. *Justification* and *new birth* mark the point where grace moves inside the circle, then becoming *sanctifying grace* (accompanied by *fruit* and *gifts*), and sin moves outside the circle, remaining as the carnal nature. Now sanctifying grace prevails, culminating (for Wesley) in a moment of entire *sanctification* or perfect love, usually just prior to physical death.

Justifying grace is the work of the Holy Spirit at the moment of conversion whereby the *process* of moving toward disobedience is stopped and the *process* of moving back toward obedience is *begun.* Note, this does not imply perfection. The plunge toward a life of disobedience has simply been reversed.

Justification is the side of conversion that denotes a *turning from* sin — what God does *for* us in Jesus Christ. It is an imputed righteousness or that which is attributed to us by virtue of our faith in Christ, a relative change.

New Birth is the side of conversion that denotes *a turning to* righteousness, what God does *in* us by the Holy Spirit. It is the *beginning of* an imparted righteousness or that which is realized in us through the power of the Holy Spirit, a real change. In most instances Wesley would have associated the outset of this transformation into the likeness of Jesus Christ (2 Cor. 3:18) with the "Baptism of the Holy Spirit."

Sanctifying grace denotes the work of the Holy Spirit in believers between conversion and death. Accompanied by fruit and gifts, sanctifying grace slowly but surely roots out those things that would separate Christians from God, themselves, and those around them.

The *fruit* of the Spirit is love, but love has characteristics such as joy, peace, patience, kindness, goodness, faithfulness, gentleness and self-control (Gal. 5:22-23). This is the only unmistakable mark of the Spirit-filled life.

The *gifts* of the Spirit are those supernatural abilities given by the Holy Spirit enabling Christians to minister effectively within their own spheres of influence. To be effective the gifts must be manifested within the context of the fruit.

Sanctification was frequently referred to by Wesley as "Entire Sanctification," or "Christian Perfection." Sanctification was usually defined as loving God with all one's heart, mind, and strength, and one's neighbor as oneself (Mark 12:29). Wesley believed one was entirely sanctified or perfected when love (the fruit) had become pure or devoid of self-interest.

Without going into further detail at this point (do not panic, each chapter will focus at the various points along this continuum so that the terms themselves serve as an outline for the book as a whole and will be described with considerable care), the chart illustrates the overall thrust of Wesley's approach to the gospel, his plan of salvation (or *ordo salutis*, if you prefer). If a text were appropriate for a book as a whole (and why not?), here it would have to be Romans 8:1-4:

> "Therefore, there is now no condemnation for those who are in Christ Jesus, because through Christ Jesus the Law of the Spirit of life set me free from the Law of sin and death. For what the Law was powerless to do in that it was weakened by the sinful nature, God did by sending his own Son in the likeness of sinful man to be a sin offering. And so he condemned sin in sinful man, in order that the righteous requirements of the Law might be fully met in us who do not live according to the sinful nature, but according to the Spirit."[2]

In fact, two of the images here provide the catalyst for our major headings. The right side of the chart is labeled the Law of Sin and Death.

The Law of Sin and Death is the Law without the Spirit, without the power nor the inclination to obey it. The result is disobedience. The propensity to sin (original sin) prevails.

The left side of the chart is labeled the Law of the Spirit of Life.

The Law of the Spirit of Life is the Law (the same Law as before) now enlivened by the Spirit so that Christians have both the power and the inclination to obey it. The result is obedience. Sanctifying grace prevails.

Where Wesley is concerned, it is important to note the connection here between Spirit and grace. As we will see in Chapter 3, the two terms are nearly synonymous in all of Wesley's writings. *A theology of grace, in fact, describes the work of the Holy Spirit from conception until death.* That is an exciting story. I am getting a bit anxious to tell it, but first, I need to speak a word of caution regarding the principles of law and grace.

Some books are easily written. Their logic is straight line. They simply remind us of what we know already. Other books are more difficult to write. Their logic is not straight line. They cut against the norm. They challenge our way of thinking and, if properly understood, can change our lives forever.

For most of the Western world, the cognitive, the rational rules supreme. The creative, the intuitive, the spiritual are for dreamers, for mystics, for saints. Most of us want something we can sink our teeth into, something that can be programmed on a computer. If it cannot be seen or heard it does not exist. We want fixed boundaries, things we can manage eight to five, so when we go home we can leave work behind and submit our brains to TV and a glass of wine.

In effect, we want law. Law seems safe, reasonable, no surprises. Law is more answer than process. It is bottom line, get-to-the-point, microwave convenience. After all, we are tired. We deserve a rest. To mow the lawn or wash the clothes is challenge enough. We scream at those who would interrupt our soap opera or football game with news of some import for world peace.

What we do not realize is that law, in and of itself, is death. There is a tired that sleep won't rest. Truth, on the other hand, sets us free, but truth will not always submit to the trend, the obvious. Its treasures, even as a process of the Spirit, are frequently captured only by waiting and listening. Since the freedom released by truth stretches the mind, it will not easily compute. Among the humanists, the secularists, the materialists, truth causes the gray matter to arc as if flirting with short circuit. Ultimately, truth yields only to grace.

Grace—now there is a word. It plumbs the depths of God. It feels awkward at first, like undressing before a lover on the wedding night, but then, it feels good because it cannot be earned, only given and received. It packs hope, peace, joy and love, yet it can seem so illusive. It is too good to be true. We do not want to be teased. We taste it, we roll it around on our tongue, swilling it around in our mouths like some tasty morsel, but too many can never quite swallow it. Our inability to digest means that we savor, but are never nourished. What a pity.

This is our dilemma. We are suspicious. Like Naaman (2 Kings 5) refusing at first to submit to Elisha's cure for leprosy (simply washing seven times in the River Jordan), it is too easy. "Logic" overrules: You get what you pay for. Where is the hook? What is the catch? Rejoice, my friends, there is no hook, there is no catch. Grace is at hand, so available, so plentiful, so free. Yet, we pack scraps for the feast.

Grace brings life. Law (to use a Wesleyan phrase), "though when ennobled [or empowered] by grace, is meet, right, and our bounden duty;" in and of itself brings death. That is the story for the telling. The difference between life and death, light and darkness, victory and defeat. God has chosen to leave those horrible options within all of us. My prayer is that God has something for you in these pages. Expect it. Perhaps on this page, or the next, you can find grace to make a choice for God and experience that God-given power—a sanctity without starch. Do not be denied. Let God arise!

Notes

1. John Wesley's *Works*, Jackson edition (14 vols.), Vol. 1, p. 256. All subsequent quotations from the *Works* of John Wesley will be taken from this edition as well, unless otherwise noted.

2. Romans 8 is the chapter of the Bible most quoted by John Wesley in his *Works*.

PART I:
THE LAW OF SIN AND DEATH

The Law of Sin and Death is the Law without the Spirit, without the power nor the inclination to obey it — the result is disobedience. The propensity to sin (original sin) prevails.

OBEDIENCE

Physical Death | Original Righteousness/ Physical Birth

Entire Sanctification

Infant Baptism

CARNAL NATURE

Actual Sin

Fruit
Gifts

SANCTIFYING GRACE PREVAILS

ORIGINAL SIN PREVAILS

THE LAW OF THE SPIRIT OF LIFE (love)

THE LAW OF SIN AND DEATH (fear)

PREVENIENT GRACE

New Birth | Justification

Justifying Grace

DISOBEDIENCE

Genesis 1:27 *Hosea 14:9*
Deuteronomy 12:25 *Colossians 3:9-10*
Psalms 25:8

> *Original righteousness is the image of God that was resident in Adam and Eve before the fall. It is a propensity to do what was right and resist what was wrong whereby immortality was at hand and fellowship with God was immanent (or near at hand) and personal.*

1. Original righteousness establishes the goal for the Spirit-filled life.
2. If original righteousness relates to the image of God, what does it mean to be created in God's own image?
3. The doctrine of original righteousness establishes the absolute necessity for the grace of God revealed in Jesus Christ.

CHAPTER
1

If this book were an airplane, Part I starts the engines and pushes back from the gate. Part II taxis and takes off. Part III reaches altitude and soars toward its destination.

Original Righteousness: in God's Own Image

Although the early chapters deal with sometimes tough (if not unfamiliar) theological concepts, a proper understanding promises significant benefits. Remember, a plane cannot become airborne if the engines have not been started. Theological concepts must be understood before we can apply them and break the bondage that would consume us. Buckle your seatbelts please.

Ever wonder how God's good creation got into such a mess? That is the story which unfolds in these first two chapters. In fact, all of Part I struggles with the Law of sin and death as an unbearable yoke. Nonetheless, this important groundwork for the book as a whole must be established.

Regardless of any particular view of creation, the Bible clearly teaches that we were created in God's own image, we lost that image, but that it can be renewed.

Gen. 1:27 reads, "So God created man in his own image, in the image of God he created him; male and female he created them." Put that with Col. 3:9-10, "Do not lie to each other, since you have taken off your old self with its practices and have put on the new self, which is being renewed in the knowledge, in the image of its Creator," and the drama builds quickly. Let's start at the beginning, however. What does it mean to be created in God's image? How is that image lost, and how can it be restored? The first question is the subject for this chapter. The subsequent questions will be addressed in the chapters to follow.

The Nature of God

Any questions concerning the created image of God necessarily begin with the nature of God. What is God really like? What is God's image that we should be made in God's likeness?

Recently, a thought came to me as I was in my seminary office talking with a student. The student was feeling guilt because she was lonely and wanted someone with whom she could share her life and ministry as mate and friend. Even though she had answered God's call and was seeking to be faithful in matters large and small, she was beginning to despair of God's willingness to grant a significant part of her heart's desire.

Perhaps, for some, the thought of being created in the image of God is not such a plus after all.

Suddenly, it occurred to me, *she thinks less of God than she does of herself.* I asked her this question: "If you were a parent and had within your power to give to your children what was truly best for them, would you spare any energy, any expense, any sacrifice?"

Her answer? "Of course not!"

I simply added, "Why would a good God be any different? If a husband is truly what is best for you, then why not expect God to bring someone into your life who can fulfill that part of your heart's desire (Ps. 103:13). Otherwise, as we seek God day by day, shouldn't we expect God to change our heart's desire? Doesn't the Psalmist say, 'May he give you the desire of your heart and make all your plans succeed' (Ps. 20:4)? Why wouldn't God be at least as loving to us as we would be to our own children (Mt. 7:11)?" I must confess that I was thinking to myself, what must we think of God?

Perhaps, for some, the thought of being created in the image of God is not such a plus after all. So, as with so many issues, there is a question behind the question. What is the nature of God really like that we should applaud God's likeness and rue the loss of it?

When considering the nature of God, I decided to use the Wesleyan ploy of bringing Scripture to bear. I turned to a complete concordance and noted just the references which begin: "God is." This is what I found.

God is merciful (Deut. 4:31; Ps. 116:5).

God is gracious and compassionate (2 Chron. 30:9).

God is faithful (1 Cor. 1:9, 10:13).

God is for us (Rom. 8:31); with us (Josh. 1:9, 3:10; 1 Sam 10:7; 1 Chron. 17:2; Is. 8:10; Zech. 8:23); in us (Phil. 2:13); among us (Josh. 3:10; Zeph. 3:17).

God is God (Deut. 7:9).

God is one God (Deut. 6:4).

God is a jealous God (Josh. 24:19).

God is our refuge (2 Sam. 22:33; Ps. 46:1, 62:8); our strength (Ps. 46:1, 73:26; Is. 12:2); our helper (Ps. 54:4); our dwelling (Deut. 33:27); our salvation (Ps. 68:19, 68:20; Is. 12:2).

God is a sun and shield (Ps. 84:11).

God is providing (Josh. 1:13).

God is giving (Josh. 1:15).

God is mighty (Job 36:5).

God is exalted in power (Job 36:22).

God is great (Job 36:26);

God is sovereign over all the earth (Ps. 47:7).

God is a righteous judge (Ps. 7:11).

God is righteous in everything done (Dan. 9:14).

God is good to the upright (Ps. 73:1).

God is holy (Ps. 99:9).

God is an everlasting rock (Is. 26:4).

God is Spirit (Jn. 4:24).

God is one (Rom. 3:30; Gal. 3:20; Jas. 2:19).

God is true (Jn. 3:33).
God is not a God of confusion (1 Cor. 14:33).
God is able to provide you with all grace (2 Cor. 9:8).
God is not ashamed to be called our God (Heb. 11:16).
God is our witness (Phil. 1:8).
God is treating us as sons [or daughters] (Heb. 12:7).
God is a consuming fire (Heb. 12:29).
God is light (1 Jn. 1:5).
God is love (1 Jn. 4:8, 4:16).

Before we continue, look back over this description of God. Who could object to such a nature or being created in such an image? Let's look a bit closer.

The Image of God

Since we are not created divine and since God's nature is obviously not complete in us, what does it mean to be created in God's image? God has at least two kinds of attributes, natural and moral. The natural attributes relate to God's omnipresence (God exists everywhere at all times), omniscience (God is all-knowing), and omnipotence (God is all-powerful).

Since you and I are not omni-anything, but fully human, even in a pre-fallen state, the image of God must necessarily relate to God's moral attributes (those remaining *within* us). These focus primarily in the areas of love and obedience. The image of God relates to our propensity to righteousness, or holiness, or more specifically, our propensity to love and obey the good and to despise and reject the bad. Recall from that earlier list of Bible passages of what God is. Righteousness was an important characteristic. This would be an area of focus for John Wesley as well.

Many believe that the image of God relates to all that distinguishes humankind from the rest of God's creation — those unique attributes which are available to the descendants of Adam and Eve. Wesley, however, understood the image of God in a much more defined sense, relating primarily to God's righteousness. On one occasion he supports this argument by quoting the following texts: Deut. 12:25, 28; 13:18; 21:9; 32:4; Ps. 25:8, 32:11, 33:1, 4; Hos. 14:9.[1] He then, however, is quick to note that the image of God's righteousness does not refer to "right action." This would be a fundamental mistake. Wesley writes that the image of God is "a right state of mind; which differs from right action, as the cause does from the effect."[2] In other words, the image of God's righteousness relates to disposition and intent (the cause), more than performance and deed (the effect). Now let's look at how the image of God relates to the doctrine of original righteousness.

Original Righteousness, Created in God's Image

Again, the Bible teaches that in the beginning humankind was created in God's own image. Wesley called that image, original righteousness. Our first parents were righteousness-prone — their innate desire for holiness made obedience easier than disobedience. Accompanying that was a fellowship with God that was immanent (or near at hand) and personal. Access to a reality beyond the senses was free and open, totally pervasive — no guilt, no shame, no fear of exposure because there was nothing to hide.

Recently I was talking with a friend who gave me an interesting insight. Loneliness is not so much caused by the fact that we do not know others, but that others do not know us, because we do not want to be known for fear of exposure. Original righteousness knows no hidden sin to be kept from the light. More will be said along these lines in a moment, but for now, note that the relevance of all this for Wesleyan theology is that this should be our expectation for the Spirit-filled life. Too many of us simply "don't know what we're missing" because we do not realize what we had.

Too many of us simply "don't know what we're missing" because we do not realize what we had.

In John Wesley's treatise *The Doctrine of Original Sin*, he has a section entitled "Original Righteousness." There (as we have done already), he explores the nature of God in an attempt to discover what it is to have that image in which we were created. The treatise itself is a defense of the doctrines of original righteousness and original sin and was drafted in response to another treatise on original sin written by an Anglican clergyman named John Taylor.

As a deist and humanist, Taylor had argued that there was no God-created original righteousness and no original sin.[3] As a deist, Taylor believed that God created us, for better or worse, merely indifferent to good or evil, and then left us alone to rise or fall. We are what we are by accident of nature to be corrupted or improved only by the influence of those around us.

As a humanist, Taylor believed that since there is no original sin, there is no need for original righteousness. Humankind could survive quite nicely without any further assistance, or (for that matter) intervention from its Creator.

Even more to the point, Taylor argued that if there were in fact an original righteousness, then how does one explain the fall? Adam must have had a sinful inclination from within which overcame his propensity to righteousness. For Wesley the answer was obvious. No, Adam's original righteousness was not overcome by a sinful inclination from within, but by a strong temptation from without.[4] Taylor made no reckoning of the forces of evil — the principalities and powers — that Wesley knew were at work in the world.

> *If our original righteousness was lost by the influence of some malevolent force, then any attempt to recover that image will require help from on high.*

The issue here is crucial. Good and evil are at war. In addition, battlelines are never drawn simply in desert sand, but in the heavenlies as well. If our original righteousness was lost by the influence of some malevolent force, then any attempt to recover that image will require help from on high.

Furthermore, if there is no original righteousness, no created image, then there is no Fall. If there is no Fall, there is no need for the grace revealed in the reconciling work of God in Jesus Christ. If there is no need for the grace revealed in the reconciling work of God in Jesus Christ, then we are without hope that God's created image will one day be restored. To say this a bit differently, if we do not understand the nature and extent of our original righteousness, then we can never understand the ways of the Enemy nor the devastation of the fall. Let's talk about that.

Whether or not you choose to acknowledge a literal Adam and Eve, the Genesis story is nonetheless of enormous importance if we are to grasp the significance of the issue before us. Wesley defines original righteousness as "'that moral rectitude in which Adam was created. His reason was clear; and sense, appetite, and passion were subject to it. His judgment was uncorrupted, and his will had a constant propensity to holiness. He had a supreme love of his Creator, a fear of offending him, and a readiness to do his will.' When Adam sinned, he lost this moral rectitude, this image of God in which he was created; in consequence of which all his posterity come into the world destitute of that image."[5]

> *Whether or not you choose to acknowledge a literal Adam and Eve, the Genesis story is nonetheless of enormous importance . . .*

Original righteousness, therefore, was universal, natural and mutable. It was universal in that everyone shares in its origin. It was natural in that everyone has hope of its restoration. It was mutable in that there was freedom to cast it aside, and so we did.

Let's put all of this in a biblical and then contemporary setting. Genesis 1 and 2 states that at some point humankind walked and talked with God. There was no "glass darkly" to prevent us from beholding the full glory of God. God was there, and our first parents knew it. The tree of life was there to enjoy even as it reappears in Revelation's heavenly vision. Adam and Eve were apparently not bound by our so-called five-dimensional world. They had access to God without the veil, without fear, without the distant promise of some mortal passing to reach that "happy shore." Original righteousness had access to heaven, then and there. Grace fulfilled the Law. The Law itself was sheer delight. It was not a burden; it was something to be enjoyed, even treasured as the key to the door eternal.

What would we give to have that original righteousness renewed, immortality at hand? That is the gospel which begins and ends with good news. The grace of God renews that righteousness whereby we can enjoy God forever. I continue to be amazed at just how some (especially the young and the elderly) seem so aware of the reality beyond, accessible not by mind or matter, but by pure and whole-hearted devotion to God.

Now for the contemporary setting. A few years ago I telephoned an old friend. The first year I taught in a theological seminary she would visit my class only to sit in the corner and pray for me the entire hour. What a marvelous gift.

As she picked up the telephone I identified myself, and she responded immediately, "The doctor just left and tells me that I am in the final stages of a melanoma, and I've only a few days to live."

"What!" I said. "What do you mean?"

"Honey, you're not hard of hearing," she replied lovingly.

"No, I'm not hard of hearing, but that's hard to hear," I said.

"It's all right," she replied. "I'm more at home with God than with this house of clay. I've got more going on beyond the veil than within it."

We talked for 10 or 15 minutes, catching up and saying goodbye before I asked, "How can I pray for you?"

"Just don't hold me back," was her only response.

I closed by praying what I call the Prayer of Enoch (don't ask me what that is, I just made it up): "God take away the pain and let my special friend walk with you a little further each day until one day soon it will be easier for her to go on home with you than to return to her temple of flesh and blood. Amen!" She died a few days later, but her original righteousness (her created image) had already been renewed. Even before her death she walked and talked with God as one sanctified (the righteousness of Jesus Christ *realized* in her) by grace through faith.

Review

Each chapter will conclude with a brief section on its relevance for understanding the way of salvation. This will also serve to coordinate a Wesleyan theology of grace.

Without original righteousness there is no Fall. Without the Fall there is no need for the grace revealed in the reconciling work of God in Jesus Christ. Without this grace, this reconciling work of

God in Jesus Christ, there is no hope for conquering those things that would keep us from God, from ourselves and from those around us. If the gospel is good news/bad news/good news, then the original good news creates the vision.

Paul Cho from South Korea says: "Describe to me your vision and I can predict your future." Proverbs 29:18 reads, "Where there is no vision, the people perish" (KJV).

God renew our vision by your grace. Renew our original right-eousness, our created image, that we may enjoy you forever.

Study Questions:

1. What is original righteousness?
2. What does it mean to be created in God's own image?
3. What important truths do we lose without such a doctrine?
4. How does the doctrine relate to good news/bad news/good news?
5. Why would such a doctrine be critical to a Wesleyan theology of grace?

Notes

[1]Wesley's *Works*, Vol. 9, p. 342. Cf. Calvin's *Institutes*, 1.15.308 for the more inclusive understanding of this doctrine.

[2]Wesley's *Works*, Vol. 9, p. 342.

[3]It would be interesting to compare Taylor's *Original Sin* with the book by Matthew Fox, *Original Blessing*. In many respects the two have a great deal in common.

[4]Wesley's *Works*, Vol. 9, pp. 344f.

[5]Wesley's *Works*, Vol. 9, p. 339.

Original Sin is a propensity to sin that resulted from the disobedience of Adam and Eve whereby they lost their propensity for righteousness, immortality at hand and the close personal fellowship with God. This became part of the human condition inherited by all subsequent generations.

1. As a result of Adam's sin a propensity for righteousness becomes a propensity for sin.

2. All subsequent generations inherit Adam's sinful nature.

3. The Law becomes a law of sin and death so that apart from grace, we are without hope in the world.

CHAPTER

2

The scene which has thus far focused on original righteousness is about to change dramatically. Although we were created in the image of God, we have lost that *imago dei* so that the Law, once a delight, is now a monstrous burden, a law of sin and death — a door leading to nowhere but fear and frustration. Again, the Genesis story is of enormous significance. Wesley writes that "the Adamic Law, that given to Adam in innocence, properly called 'the Law of works,'" since his "body was then no clog to the mind," was fully attainable.[1] Now, however, as a result of the fall, the very nature of our being has changed. Adam's mortality has been transmuted to all future generations. Rather than prone to good, we are prone to evil. That is the tragic story to be told here under the following headings: the Covenant (or Law) of Works, the Fall, Original Sin Defined, and The Law of Sin and Death.

Original Sin: a Propensity to Disobedience

The Covenant (or Law) of Works

Briefly, let's set the stage once more, this time from a slightly different perspective. Original righteousness implies a covenant or law given to humankind before the fall. Wesley explains that "consequently, this Law, proportioned to his [Adam's] original powers, required that he should always think, always speak, and always act precisely right, in every point whatsoever. He was able to do so: And God could not but require the service he was able to pay."[2] Simply stated, this covenant or law was instituted before the Fall and it consisted of the promise of eternal life for obedience and the threat of death for disobedience.[3]

> *The difference between the covenant (or law) of works and the subsequent covenants (those established after the Fall) is that this earliest covenant, as Wesley reminded us, was entirely achievable.*

Again, the difference between the covenant (or law) of works and the subsequent covenants (those established after the Fall) is that this earliest covenant, as Wesley reminded us, was entirely achievable. All of this was soon to alter permanently so that *none* of the covenants following could possibly be fulfilled apart from the grace of God available through faith in the Promise. For Abraham and those before the coming of Christ, that would be faith in the Promise to come (Heb. 11:13). For us and those since the coming of Christ, that would be faith in the Promise fulfilled (Mt. 12:17-21). The obedience, death and resurrection of Jesus Christ stand at the center of salvation history as the fulfillment of God's Promise to remedy the brokenness of the fall (Rom. 5:12-21).

The Fall

There is no greater tragedy to be described. Our first parents had only to enjoy fellowship with God in a setting which met their every need. There was no limit to things now unavailable to the senses. The heavenly dimension was a reality readily perceived. The tree of life was there. There was but one condition if all of this was to be enjoyed forever. Eat of any of the trees except from the tree of knowledge of good and evil. Evil itself, disguised as a serpent, is depicted in conversation with Eve. Listen carefully to the lie, the incredible lie, perhaps the greatest lie of all.

Now the serpent was more crafty than any of the wild animals the Lord God had made. He said to the woman, "Did God really say, 'you must not eat from any tree in the garden'?"

The woman said to the serpent, "We may eat fruit from the trees in the garden, but God did say, 'You must not eat fruit from the tree that is in the middle of the garden, and you must not touch it, or you will die.'"

"You will not surely die," the serpent said to the woman. "For God knows that when you eat of it your eyes will be opened, and you will be like God, knowing good and evil." (Gen. 3:1-5)

When Adam and Eve ate the fruit they did indeed receive knowledge, but they did not become like God . . . they became totally, if not horribly, aware of the contrast between God and God's creation.

When Adam and Eve ate the fruit they did indeed receive knowledge, but they did not become like God. They became only aware of their own nakedness. As created beings, they became totally, if not horribly, aware of the contrast between God and God's creation. They became aware that original righteousness does not give access to those natural attributes available only to God as Creator.

Although creation is good, it is not divine. In fact, our freedom, intended for obedience, if used for disobedience, would subvert those moral attributes that we had already. Thus, Satan's lie was a veritable masterpiece of deceit, brewed in some malevolent cauldron, heated by the fires of hell, deep within the bowels of torment.

If one is looking for a proper metaphor, imagine seeing something for the first time, not knowing what it is, and describe it in terms already understood. In this instance (and who can truly fathom the depths of such deceit), it seems as if Satan is telling Adam and Eve that they could fly, then lures their wingless forms into the flames as they are goaded into leaping from some lofty pinnacle. As the leap was made, suddenly the reality, the knowledge hits them — we cannot fly. We have no wings, no special power. Our disobedience has doomed us to imminent death. Little wonder they ran for cover. That God should see their foolishness would be too much to bear. Pride comes before the fall, indeed! The pride was great, but greater still the fall.

> *The Garden was taken away as our senses, once attuned to the eternal, would now readily submit only to a purely physical world . . .*

Contemporary illustrations of just how this same scene is reenacted abound. Humanism tells us we must get along on our own. The truth is, we must not. Materialism tells we cannot get along without lots of things. The truth is, we can. Secularism tells us that we can get along without God. The truth is, we cannot. Individualism or even certain types of nationalism tells us that we can get along without others. The truth is, we cannot. Agnosticism says that the existence of God does not really matter. The truth is, it does. Atheism says that God does not exist. The truth is, God does exist, the Rose of Sharon, the Lion of Judah, the Alpha and Omega, forever and forever.

Original Sin Defined

In one sense, original sin could be defined simply as the Fall, the sin of Adam and Eve which is then imputed to us through their fallen nature. Since this definition (as we will see in a moment) still leaves some unanswered questions, let's walk it through step by step.

As a result of the Fall, our nature has been permanently altered. The Garden was taken away as our senses, once attuned to the eternal, would now readily submit only to a purely physical world where everything else could be seen only as a "poor reflection" (1 Cor. 13:12). The flesh suddenly hung more heavily upon the bone. Our metaphysical system was confined to the five-dimensional box (height, width, depth, time and motion) of this world sensation. The free and open association where we walk and talk with God (except perhaps by the dispensation of a special anointing for the lonely prophet such as Jonah or Ezekiel), was gone. The bliss of ready provision, gone, replaced by sweat and toil. Painless childbirth, gone. The promise of eternal life, gone. The tree of life (not to be seen or even heard of again until a possible reference in Ezekiel 47:12 or, more definitively, the Apostle John's heavenly vision in Revelation 22), gone, since to eat of this fruit (with-

The flesh suddenly hung more heavily upon the bone.

out the reconciliation available through Jesus Christ) would serve only to perpetuate the agony of our fallen state.

Original sin has been described in several different ways and Wesley himself seems to flirt with at least two definitions not altogether compatible (proof once again that Wesley was no martyr to the bugbear of consistency).

Reformed theology (that which emphasizes the sovereign foreknowledge of God and predestination) speaks of original sin in terms of total depravity; that is, an inherent corruption extending to every part of our natures so that everyone "is as thoroughly depraved as he can possibly become."[4] At one point Wesley seems to follow this lead as he describes his own condition prior to his experience on Aldersgate Street: "I 'am fallen short of the glory of God': (seeing it cannot be, that a 'evil tree' should 'bring forth good fruit':) That 'alienated' as I am from the life of God, I am 'a child of wrath' an heir of hell."[5]

In order to explain the root of such corruption, Wesley refers specifically to the result of Adam's sin:

> His understanding, originally enlightened with wisdom, was clouded with ignorance [so much for the theory taught by some that Wesley believed that humankind was cor-

rupted only from the neck down, leaving the mind free to reason its way to God]. His heart, once warmed with heavenly love, became alienated from God his Maker. His passions and appetites, rational and regular before, shook off the government of order and reason. In a word, the whole moral frame was unhinged, disjointed, broken. . . . By this 'one man's sin entered into the world, and passed upon all men': and through the infection which they derived from him, all men are and ever were, by nature, entirely 'alienated from the life of God; without hope, without God in the world."[6]

Contrast with this Wesley's discussion of original sin in reaction to John Taylor, who, as we noted in Chapter 1, denied both original righteousness and original sin. There Wesley says we derive from Adam "a moral taint and infection, whereby we have a natural propensity to sin."[7] It would appear that here Wesley is not arguing for original sin as total depravity so much as for original sin as a propensity, a proneness to sin which could be resisted (Christ did), but we do not, so that actual sin (see Chapter 5) results, corrupting our entire nature and making it totally impossible to save ourselves.

> *Wesley, in effect, believed that we are not condemned for original sin (that is, a propensity to sin) alone, but that we are condemned for original sin plus actual sin.*

The shift here might seem subtle, but it is important. Wesley writes, "All have a natural propensity to sin. Nevertheless, this propensity is not necessary, if by necessary you mean irresistible. We can resist and conquer it, too, by the grace [prevenient grace, see Chapter 3] which is ever at hand."[8] Two concepts surface here that will be discussed at length in Chapters 3 and 5, prevenient grace (the Spirit at work upon us between conception and conversion) and actual (or willful) sin. The import at the present, however, is that Wesley, in effect, believed that we are not condemned for original sin (that is, a propensity to sin) alone, but that we are condemned for original sin *plus* actual sin.

I remember when our last child was born. I actually saw her while she was still in her mother. When the doctor showed her to us immediately after delivery my wife and I both thought that she was so perfect she would not have to be baptized. Wrong! Within seconds she was screaming as if to say, "Feed me *now!*" Suddenly the entire universe revolved around her mouth. Psychologists have a name for that, narcissism. Bonhoeffer called it sin: "Life was intended to be lived *from* the center with God as our center, not *at* the center with ourselves as the center." John Wesley called it (for those who continued to sin willfully) atheism, quoting the well known line, "Myself am king of me."[9] By nature we become our own God.

> *"Life was intended to be lived* from *the center with God as our center, not* at *the center with ourselves as the center."*

Although a few years ago my daughter matured to the place where she exchanged the kind of a world where she was at its center for the kind of a world where God was at its center, it was her faith and trust in Jesus Christ that worked the change. Admittedly, original sin had moved her out of orbit with "the God who is God," but original sin alone did not condemn her. Again, original sin plus actual sin brought the condemnation and placed her in need of a Savior.

One more quotation from Wesley should underscore this point before moving on to the next section,

> Perhaps you will say, They are not condemned for actual, but for original sin. What do you mean by this term? The inward corruption of our nature? If so, it has been spoken of before. Or, do you mean the sin which Adam committed in paradise? That this is imputed to all men, I allow; yea, that by reason hereof 'the whole creation groaneth and travaileth in pain together until now.' But that any would be damned for this alone, I allow not, till he show

where it is written. Bring me plain proof from Scripture, and I submit; but till then I utterly deny it.[10]

The Law of Sin and Death

In the chart presented in the Introduction we saw the contrast between the law of the Spirit of life and the law of sin and death. The explanatory notes there defined the law of sin and death as the Law without the Spirit, without the power nor the inclination to obey it. As a result of the Fall the first covenant was no longer workable. Although subsequent covenants or laws were established where grace (prevenient grace) was made available, our sin proneness made failure all but inevitable. Although Adam's sin might not have been imputed in the sense that our condemnation lies on the head of someone else, our propensity to sin leads to actual sin whereby we are judged for our own disobedience to a law which (without the Spirit) serves only to condemn.

Wesley epitomizes subsequent covenants (or laws) with the covenant established with Moses. The Law of Moses had three parts — the political, the ceremonial (or ritual) and the moral. Although the Law as political and ceremonial functioned as a sort of a shadowy precursor to Christ, and by virtue of *his* obedience, death and resurrection he did away with those parts of the Law, the moral Law still stands. Wesley quotes the words of Jesus: "'Think not that I am come to destroy' or abolish 'the Law: I am not come to destroy, but to fulfill.'"[11]

> *Wesley was consistently at odds with those who would attempt to disregard the Law altogether.*

Wesley was consistently at odds with those who would attempt to disregard the Law altogether. On one such occasion a person quoted Galatians 3:13, "Christ hath redeemed us from the curse of the Law, being made a curse for us," and Wesley responded, "'Christ hath redeemed us' (all that believed) 'from the curse' or punishment, justly due to our past transgressions of God's Law. But it speaks not a word of redeeming us from the Law, anymore than from love or heaven."[12]

Nonetheless, the point is still well taken. Apart from the power of the Spirit available through faith in Christ, the Law, even the moral law, is still unreachable. Although Jesus, himself subject to Adam's propensity to sin, overcame temptation with far less advantage than Adam (if you believe that Jesus was fully human as well as fully God), our lot has been what seems to be inevitable disobedience. Jesus Christ, tempted as we are tempted (Heb. 2), resisted temptation, ensuring salvation for those who would trust his efficacy and receive his Holy Spirit. More about that is to come, but for now the issue is clear. The Law is unreachable. Rom. 3:23: "All have sinned and fallen short of God's glory." Let's look even closer by way of a brief analogy.

> *Apart from the power of the Spirit available through faith in Christ, the Law, even the moral law, is still unreachable.*

The Law without the Spirit, available through faith in Jesus Christ, is death. It requires perfect obedience of a "stiff-necked people," unwilling to obey God and resist temptation. That is like requiring a four-minute mile from those ill-prepared for the rigors of conditioning. Although the intent of the Law is good, the end is death. In short, Law is no longer a delight. It is a burden impossible to bear. *Kyrie Eleison* (Lord, have mercy.).

Review

Perhaps the relevance of original sin for understanding the way of salvation and a Wesleyan theology of grace can best be described as we allow Wesley to speak for himself.

First: "Our fall, corruption, and apostasy in Adam, has been the reason why the Son of God came into the world, and 'gave himself a ransom' for us."[13]

Second: "Because we are 'born in sin;' nature is adverse to all good, and inclined to all evil: Therefore, we must be born again, before we can please God."[14]

Third: "'But what good end does this doctrine promote?' The doctrine, that we are by nature 'dead in sin,' and therefore 'children of wrath,' promotes repentance, a true knowledge of ourselves; and thereby leads to faith in Christ, to a true knowledge of Christ crucified."[15]

To whet your appetites a bit for what is to come in Parts II and III, know that Christ fulfilled the Law, making available to us his Holy Spirit so that the Law will not always be a Law of sin and death. Furthermore, the beginning of what God can do by the Spirit is already at work, and that is the part of the story that we turn to now.

Study Questions

1. What is original sin?
2. What is the difference between the covenant (or law) of works and all subsequent covenants?
3. What is the significance of the Fall?
4. How do the covenant (or law) of works and the Fall relate to the law of sin and death?
5. Can you identify some of the effects of original sin in our world today?

Notes

[1] Wesley's *Works*, Vol. 11, p. 414.

[2] Wesley's *Works*, Vol. 11, p. 415.

[3] Johannes Wollebius and William Ames, two seventeenth-century theologians, pioneered the various concepts of CovenantTheology which begin with a covenant of (law or) works.

[4] L. Berkhof, *Systematic Theology*, pp. 246f.

[5] Wesley's *Works*, Vol. 1, p. 76.

[6] Wesley's *Works*, Vol. 9, pp. 242, 258. For further study cf. Vol. 6, pp. 54ff.; and Wesley's sermon on "Original Sin."

[7] Wesley's *Works*, Vol. 9, p. 293.

[8] Wesley's *Works*, Vol. 9, p. 294.

[9] Wesley's *Works*, Vol. 7, p. 89.

[10]Wesley's *Works*, Vol. 10, p. 223.

[11]Wesley's *Works*, Vol. 5, p. 311; cf. Vol. 5, pp. 433f.

[12]Wesley's *Works*, Vol. 10, p. 271.

[13]Wesley's *Works*, Vol. 9, p. 302.

[14]Wesley's *Works*, Vol. 9, p. 308.

[15]Wesley's *Works*, Vol. 9, p. 312.

Psalms 22:9-10　　Luke 1:15
Isaiah 49:1　　　　Acts 16:14
Jeremiah 1:5

Prevenient grace is the Holy Spirit at work in everyone between conception and conversion. The Holy Spirit woos or prevents *us from moving so far toward disobedience, that when we finally understand the claims of the gospel upon our lives, we are guaranteed the freedom to say yes.*

1. Grace (according to John Wesley) is defined as the work of the Holy Spirit throughout the world.

2. Prevenient grace, therefore, is the Holy Spirit at work in everyone between conception and conversion.

3. This grace is at work in everyone the world over preparing them for the ministry of the church.

CHAPTER

3

Someone has said, "None can harm him who does not harm himself." The problem is, we have harmed ourselves, fatally. "'Every one of us,' by the corruption of our inmost nature, 'is very far gone from original righteousness'; so far, that 'every person born into the world deserveth God's wrath and damnation'; that we have *by nature* no power either to help ourselves, or even to call upon God to help us . . . ."[1] A part of that story has already been told. Original righteousness succumbs to the Fall so that our only expectation for salvation is that God somehow mercifully intervene. We are out of orbit with God, powerless to change. Yet, Wesley insists that we can be restored to the "whole image of God."[2] How can that happen?

In Mark 10:24-25 Jesus seems to describe the Kingdom of God as almost inaccessible. Then, just as the disciples begin to despair he says these words: "With man this is impossible, but not with God; all things are possible with God" (Mark 10:27). *With God*, that is the

Prevenient Grace: God's Initiative in the Drama of Rescue

key. In the drama of rescue God willingly plays the principal role. God's initiative (after all we love God because God *first* loved us) in the miracle of our salvation is the work of the Spirit in prevenient grace.

The seventeenth-century Scotsman, Henry Scougal, wrote a book entitled *The Life of God in the Soul of Man*. There Scougal describes the work of the Spirit from cradle to grave. That book was so important that Wesley included an abridgement of it in his own published works. The eighteenth-century evangelist George Whitefield states that this was the book that led him to faith in Jesus Christ. Perhaps it is time for another more systematic approach to the work of the Spirit in the life of a Christian from conception to death that does not remove the issues solely to the academic cloister.

John Wesley states that God begins a work in each of us while we are still in the womb. Jeremiah prophesies, "Before I formed you in the womb I knew you, before you were born I set you apart" (Jeremiah 1:5). Luke records that John the Baptist would "be filled with the Holy Spirit even from birth" (Luke 1:15). In fact, the term "prevenient grace" quite simply refers to the work of the Spirit *in all of us* prior to conversion. We will discuss this important doctrine under the following headings: The Spirit Connection, Prevenient Grace Defined and The Doctrine Applied.

The Spirit Connection

Again, as with many theological issues, there is a question behind the question. Before we can discuss Wesley's understanding of prevenient (or preventing) grace, we must first of all discuss his understanding of grace itself.

We have already mentioned, just in passing, that grace for Wesley is nearly synonymous with the work of the Holy Spirit. The terms "prevenient," "justifying," and "sanctifying grace" are simply different ways of describing the work of the Spirit at various points in the life of the Christian. In his sermon, "The Witness of Our Own Spirit," Wesley writes that "by *'the grace of God'* is sometimes to be understood that free love, that unmerited mercy, by which I a sinner, through the merits of Christ, am now reconciled to God. But in this place *it rather means that power of God, the Holy Ghost, which 'worketh in us both to will and to do of His good pleasure.'"*[3] John

Fletcher, Wesley's appointed successor had Wesley not outlived him, makes the same identification between grace and Spirit.[4]

In fact, Fletcher attempted to get Wesley to use the language of the Spirit more openly but (I suspect) Wesley, in an age when even the mention of the Spirit was frequently hammered as rank "enthusiasm," chose to disguise much of his own language of the Spirit (but by no means all) with the language of grace. For now, however, the association between grace and Spirit is certain.[5] So, what does all this mean?

Prevenient Grace Defined

Prevenient grace has been commonly referred to as that work of God in the life of the believer (or at least potential believer) between conception and conversion. If our identification of grace with Spirit is legitimate, then what we are really talking about is *the work of the Holy Spirit* in the life of the believer between conception and conversion.

Prevenient grace was, of course, not a term unique to John Wesley. In fact, I do not recall that he ever used the term, as such, opting for the words "preventing grace" as preparatory for the more narrowly defined *convincing grace* and *repentance* to follow. Wesley write,: "Salvation begins with what is usually termed (and very properly) *preventing grace*, including the first wish to please God, the first dawn of light concerning his will, and the first slight transient conviction of having sinned against him. All these imply some tendency toward life, some degree of salvation, the beginning of a deliverance from a blind, unfeeling heart, quite insensible of God and the things of God. Salvation is carried on by *convincing grace*, usually in Scripture termed *repentance*, which brings a larger measure of self-knowledge, and a farther deliverance from the heart of stone."[6]

> *Prevenient grace has been commonly referred to as that work of God in the life of the believer (or at least potential believer) between conception and conversion.*

The actual term "prevenient grace" was probably first coined by Augustine. Then the theologians of the old Franciscan School referred to prevenient grace as the "law" which convicted and thereby prepared one for "real grace" which came only through the sacraments. The Reformers objected. Luther, in particular, regarded the whole medieval conception of grace as too narrow, a degradation, or at best, a misapplication, of the Word of God. The Reformation bias insisted that grace (or God's unmerited favor) was imparted, not simply through the "law," but through the entire Word of God — the Scriptures. We should not, therefore, find it surprising that the Spirit was also tied very closely to, if not bound by, the Scriptures.

To broaden our scope just a bit, listen to the words of John Calvin. He writes that while Paul

> urges the Thessalonians not to 'quench the Spirit' (1 Thessalonians 5:19-20), [he] does not loftily catch them up to empty speculations without the Word . . . . Certainly a far different sobriety befits the children of God, who just as they see themselves, without the Spirit of God bereft of the whole light of truth, so are not unaware that *the Word is the instrument by which the Lord dispenses the illumination of His Spirit* to believers.[7]

Wesley, although no doubt aware of Calvin's admonition, expanded his own understanding of grace even beyond that of the Reformers to include *any work of the Spirit, by whatever means*, in the life of the believer. Furthermore, Calvin not only limited the Spirit's work to the Scriptures, he insisted that the quickening of the Word of God, and thereby the Spirit, was imparted only to the *elect*. This, of course, limited prevenient grace (or "special" grace according to Calvin) to those predestined or foreordained to become a convenant people and, by the same logic, denied prevenient grace to those who were somehow passed by. The effect of all this was that some were apparently "chosen" for heaven, others for hell. To Wesley this made God appear arbitrary. He would have none of it.

In his treatise "Predestination Calmly Considered" Wesley argues,

> But you [the Calvinists] know in your own conscience, God might justly have passed by you:' I deny it. That God might justly, for my unfaithfulness to his [prevenient] grace,

have given me up long ago, I grant: But his concession supposes me to have had that [prevenient] grace which you say a reprobate never had.[8]

Wesley seems to have emphasized *his* understanding of prevenient grace in contrast to an opposing Calvinism which determined to preserve the sovereignty of God in all of salvation (admittedly a worthy task), but dispensed with the freedom of human response. Again, to state it simply, Calvin and many of the Reformed theologians to follow spoke of prevenient grace as that special grace *limited and available only to the elect*. It was *irresistible*. Wesley, on the other hand, spoke of prevenient grace as that preventing grace universal and available to all. It was *resistible*.

> *Wesley insisted that salvation "from the first dawning of grace in the soul, till it is consumated in glory" was the work of God.*

Wesley insisted that salvation "from the first dawning of grace in the soul, till it is consumated in glory" was the work of God. He writes that the work of salvation includes

all that is wrought in the soul by what is frequently termed "natural conscience" [or common grace for Calvin], but more properly, preventing grace; — all the drawings of the Father; the desires after God, which, if we yield to them, increase more and more; — all that light wherewith the Son of God "enlighteneth everyone that cometh into the world . . . ."[10]

In light of all of this, Wesley might have argued thusly. Prevenient grace describes the Spirit of God calling us while still in our mother's womb, who from our birth has made mention of our name (Is. 49:1; cf. Ps. 22:9-10). It describes the Spirit who gently moves our wills, who draws and woos us, as it were, to walk in the light.[11] It describes the "hound of heaven" stalking, if not courting, us between conception and conversion, preventing us from moving so far from the way (or toward disobedience) that when we finally understand the claims of the Gospel upon our lives, the Spirit of God guarantees our freedom to say yes.

The Doctrine Applied

For Wesley the doctrine of prevenient grace served at least two primary purposes. *First*, it preserved the integrity of our own freedom and of a human response. It guaranteed the validity of an evangelistic appeal. Since prevenient grace is universal, the Holy Spirit is at work guaranteeing that every man, woman and child the world over has an equal opportunity to respond, if not to the name, at least to the person of Jesus Christ.

> *"Here are you, a sinner, convinced that you deserve the damnation of Hell. Sorrow, therefore, and fear have filled your heart. And how shall you be comforted?"*

Again, in his "Predestination Calmly Considered," Wesley objects to Calvinism just along these lines. He offers this challenge.

Make the case your own: Here are you, a sinner, convinced that you deserve the damnation of Hell. Sorrow, therefore, and fear have filled your heart. And how shall you be comforted? By the promises of God? But perhaps you have no part therein; for they belong only to the elect. By the consideration of His love and tender mercy? But what are these to you, if you are a reprobate? God does not love you at all; you, like Esau, he hath hid it even from eternity. What ground then can you have for the least shadow of hope? Why, it is possible (that is all,) that God's sovereign will may be on your side. Possibly God may save you, because He will! Oh poor encouragement to despairing sinners! I fear "faith" rarely "cometh by hearing" this![12]

Second, Wesley's doctrine of prevenient grace gave God the initiative in the drama of rescue. In his sermon, "Working Out Our

Salvation," he writes, "God worketh in you; therefore, you *can* work: Otherwise it would be impossible. If He did not work, it would be impossible for you to work out your own salvation . . . ."[13] Without God's prevenient grace our answer to the gospel claim upon our lives would be inevitably, NO! By God's prevenient grace we can at least say, YES!

Wesley, in that same sermon, goes on to argue that this same grace insures our accountability before God. Though we are dead in sin (without even the notion of "natural conscience," mistakenly defended by Calvin as "common grace," for Wesley there was no such thing), God's Holy Spirit quickens enough "good desires" (though most stifle them before they can bear fruit) so that "everyone has some measure of that light, some faint glimmering ray, which sooner or later, more or less, enlightens every man that cometh into the world . . . so that no man sins because he has not grace, but because he does not use the grace which he hath."[14] Here we can see clearly a prevenient grace which is both resistible and universal.

Not to belabor the point, but in spite of Wesley's insistence that our freedom, and in fact, our responsibility to respond, was the result of God's sovereign initiative, the Calvinists were still not satisfied. He was continually labeled a "Pelagian" for "robbing God of His glory in man's salvation." Contrary to Wesley, Pelagius taught that there was no original sin and we could, therefore, work out our own salvation apart from the grace of God — a works-righteousness. The Calvinists insisted that one must hold to election (heaven for the elect and, as the natural consequence, hell for the rest) or yield to free-will.

> *[Wesley] was continually labeled a "Pelagian" for "robbing God of His glory in man's salvation."*

Wesley countered these charges by insisting (interestingly enough) that he did not carry free-will as far as they did. Once again in his "Predestination Calmly Considered," he argues importantly: "Natural free-will, in the present state of mankind, I do not understand: I only assert, that there is a measure of free-will *supernaturally* restored to every man, together with that *supernatural* light which 'enlightens every man that cometh into the world.'"[15] Wesley then concludes (and this is equally important) that "God nevertheless may have all the glory. Why, the very power to 'work together with him was from God.'"[16]

Again, to put all of this just a bit differently, prevenient grace is that work of the Holy Spirit, supernaturally restoring all of us, by whatever means, to a measure of free-will by reminding us, convicting us, warning us, promising us, inviting us, waiting for us. *It is God's initiative guaranteeing the freedom of our own response.* In an age when much of our teaching and preaching smacks once again of works-righteousness (associating salvation only with that which we do, disregarding the crucial ingredients — by grace through faith) this is a vital corrective. Like Karl Barth to follow, John Wesley puts God back on the throne of grace, back in the lead role in the drama of rescue. Surely, "we love God because God *first* loved us." Indeed, we are more "known than knowing." Let me illustrate.

> *Where would you be without the influence of that special "saint" used of God as a means of grace for the moving of the power of the Holy Spirit in your life?*

Few lives demonstrate the importance of prevenient grace more effectively than the life of John Wesley. In a biography on John Wesley written some years ago, and more recently in a book *Mysticism in the Wesleyan Tradition*, time and again I sought to illustrate just how powerfully God was at work in Wesley's life long before either his "religious" (1725) or his "evangelical" (1738) conversion. Wesley's home environment, his early training, a "religious friend," the Holy Club, the Moravians were all just a few of the instruments of God's prevenient grace. For example, in his Journal for Tuesday, March 7, 1738, Wesley writes, "(A day much to be remembered.) At the house of Mr. Weinantz, a Dutch merchant, I met Peter Bohler . . . ." Peter Bohler, you remember, eventually led Wesley, virtually by the hand, to Aldersgate (where his heart was "strangely warmed").

Let's get closer to home. Where would *you* be without the influence of that special "saint" (perhaps a mother or father, a neighbor, a godly man or woman down the street, a church school teacher or pastor), used of God as a means of grace for the moving of the power of the Holy Spirit in your life?

Some years ago I saw a man give his life to Christ. Soon afterwards he said to me, "I've been thinking. It seems to me that it takes an average of at least 25 different witnesses before any real encounter with God takes place and just because you were number 25, you think you did it all." He was right! God forgive me! I did think that I had done it all because I did not then understand prevenient grace. Those who understand the principles of prevenient grace receive just as much affirmation in being 1 – 24 (or 26 – 50 for that matter) as in being number 25. Remember that.

> *Prevenient grace is at work even at this moment preparing people for our ministry.*

It is also important to realize that prevenient grace is at work even at this moment preparing people for our ministry. **God truly has more invested in our ministry than we do!** If prevenient grace is universal, then the Spirit of God is already taking the initiative in the salvation of all of those who will believe. Our task is simply to be faithful to those within our sphere of influence knowing that God has called us to a ministry of reconciliation (2 Cor. 5:16-21). I have always liked that passage in Acts 16:14 where Luke tells us that "the Lord opened her [Lydia's] heart to respond to Paul's message." The prevenient grace of God was already at work in Lydia, a dealer in purple, preparing her heart to receive the gospel of truth. It is good to know that our ministry is simply to move into the stream of God's already intercession (where God is already at work). We are not in it alone. God, in effect, has delivered the whole world into the hands of the church. That should make us bold. How long before we "walk out the land"?

Review

Let's put all of this within the context of the overall schema outlined in our introductory chart. Prevenient grace seeks to counter the effects of original sin, preventing us from moving so far toward disobedience that when we finally understand the claims of the gospel upon our lives the Holy Spirit guarantees our freedom to say "yes." It is resistible, yet universal.

Equally important, even as you read these lines the Spirit of God is at work within your sphere of influence preparing someone for your specific ministry. If the telephone rings, thank God for an opportunity to move into the stream of God's already intercession.

Before reading further, briefly review our chart and notice that there are two points labeled "infant baptism" and "actual sin." Although these are the topics for the next two chapters, it is important to note here (as we anticipate those chapters) that it is my strong conviction that the sacraments accelerate the power of grace, the Holy Spirit. In the case of infant baptism, for example, this is obviously *prevenient* grace working to sustain the child so that the effects of actual sin are not so devastating. Make sense? Let's look more closely.

Study Questions:

1. What is the connection between the Holy Spirit and grace?
2. What is prevenient grace?
3. What is the relevance for a doctrine of "free will?"
4. How does this doctrine affect our ministry today?
5. How can this doctrine enable you to encourage others?

Notes

[1]Wesley's *Standard Journal*, Curnock ed., Vol. 2, pp. 249.

[2]Wesley's *Standard Letters*, Telford ed., Vol. 5, p. 215.

[3]Wesley's *Works*, Vol. 5, p. 141 (italics mine); cf. Vol. 5, p. 106.

[4]Fletcher's *Works*, Benson ed., Vol. 8, p. 464. Cf. p. 465 where Fletcher exhorts believers: "You want fresh baptism, till the Holy Ghost, *which is grace*, fills your soul" (italics mine). We will come

back to Fletcher later on when discussing the work of the Holy Spirit in sanctification where Fletcher makes a significant contribution.

[5] Cf. Wesley's *Works*, Vol. 9, p. 103 and Vol. 14, p. 355.

[6] Wesley's *Works*, Vol. 6, p. 509.

[7] Calvin's *Institutes*, 1.ix3 (italics mine).

[8] Wesley's *Works*, Vol. 10, p. 217.

[9] Wesley's *Works*, Vol. 6, p. 44.

[10] Wesley's *Works*, Vol. 6, p. 44.

[11] Wesley's *Works*, Vol. 10, pp. 232f.

[12] Wesley's *Works*, Vol. 10, pp. 220f.; cf. Vol. 10, p. 223.

[13] Wesley's *Works*, Vol. 6, p. 512.

[14] Wesley's *Works*, Vol. 6, p. 512.

[15] Wesley's *Works*, Vol. 10, p. 230 (italics mine).

[16] Wesley's *Works*, Vol. 10, p. 230.

Matthew 3:15
Acts 2:38; 22:16
Romans 6:3-4
1 Corinthians 1:17

Ephesians 4:5
Colossians 2:11-12
Titus 3:5
1 Peter 3:21

Infant baptism is the sacrament in which the infant children of Christian parents are baptized (one hopes within a community of believers) so that the effects of prevenient grace are accelerated and the devastation of actual sin diminished.

1. Generally speaking a sacrament is any rite or act instituted by Christ himself for the good of the church. More specifically a sacrament is an outward and visible sign of an inward and spiritual *grace*.

2. The sacrament of infant baptism is then discussed from several Wesleyan perspectives.

3. The importance of such an experience for the children of Christian believers is emphasized.

CHAPTER

4

Before weighing the full effects of original sin as they culminate in the condemnation that accompanies actual sin (chapter 5), there is another chapter to be written alongside the discussion of prevenient grace, infant baptism.

Infant Baptism: Grace Accelerated

Over the past years controversies have raged around the church's understanding of baptism. One extreme has its babies "sprinkled," merely as a rite of passage. Another extreme insists on adult baptism by immersion as the only legitimate practice. There *is* middle ground which takes the sacrament seriously, but makes it available to infants as well. Let's set the stage properly.

Although prevenient grace is resistible (or at least not irresistible, as argued within the Reformed tradition), it does guarantee our freedom to say "yes" as we begin to understand the claims of the gospel upon our lives. Unfortunately, original sin (that propensity to sin) has already accomplished its work and the damage is done. To disobey God willfully past the time when we consciously understand the difference between right and wrong compounds our separation from God. More will be said about that in our next chapter, but for now it is good to know that there is something that can be done within the Christian family so that the effects of actual sin are not so devastating. That is the role of infant baptism. Let's discuss this important doctrine under the following headings: A Sacrament Defined; Infant Baptism, as Described by John Wesley; Some Possible Scenarios in Understanding Wesley's Description; and The Doctrine Applied.

A Sacrament Defined

Broadly speaking, classical Christian theology has quite simply defined a sacrament as any rite or act instituted by Christ himself for the good of the Church. The Roman Catholics list seven (penance, confirmation, ordination, healing/Unction, marriage, Holy Communion/Eucharist, and baptism).[1] Although there might be some merit in including at least healing and marriage (if marriage is not a sacrament, it might well ought to be), Protestants generally acknowledge only two, Holy Communion (or Eucharist) and baptism.

More specifically, the Church has defined sacrament as an outward and visible sign of an inward and spiritual *grace*. Although the second/third century African church father Tertullian first introduced the term "sacrament" to Christian vocabulary as a means of underscoring the obligatory relationship between God and God's people; it was Augustine who first attempted to give the term a precise definition.

Augustine closely tied his understanding of the term "sacrament" to his doctrine of grace. Although distinguishing between the "external action" (*signum*) and the "divine inner operation of grace" (*res*), the two were inextricably bound through faith in Christ and the Word (*Verbum*) that constituted them. The effect of all this was to establish the necessity of the sacraments for salvation. No sacraments meant no church, and there was no salvation outside the church.

John Wesley's "An Earnest Appeal to Men of Reason and Religion" cites three things as essential to the Church.

> First: Living faith; without which, indeed, there can be no church at all, neither visible nor invisible. Secondly: Preaching, and consequently hearing, the pure word of

God, else that faith would languish and die. And, Thirdly,
a due administration of the sacraments,— *the ordinary
means whereby God increaseth faith*.[2]

It is the phrase, "whereby God increaseth faith," that supplies the
catalyst for that part of our chapter heading, "Grace Accelerated."
Let me explain.

Although Wesley speaks no definitive word on the sacraments
(as will be explained shortly), it seems apparent to me that both
baptism and the Eucharist accelerate the effects of grace, the work of
the Holy Spirit (cf. Acts 2:38; 1 Cor. 11:26). For example, since
Wesley understood Holy Communion as a converting as well as a
confirming sacrament, Holy Communion would accelerate the effects of justifying (or perhaps even prevenient) and sanctifying grace.
Relevant to this Wesley writes,

> What is to be inferred from this undeniable matter of
> fact — one that had not faith received it in the Lord's
> Supper? Why: (1) that there are means of grace — that is,
> outward ordinances — whereby the inward grace of God
> is ordinarily conveyed to man, whereby the faith that brings
> salvation is conveyed to them who before had it not; (2)
> that one of these means is the Lord's Supper; and (3) that
> he who has not this faith ought to wait for it in the use of
> both this and of the other means which God hath or-
> dained.[3]

From this and many other similar quotations it is clear that
Wesley believed that the Holy Spirit's work is miraculously focused
in the sacraments so that the believer (or potential believer) is brought
or elevated to a higher level of grace or communion with Jesus
Christ himself.

Furthermore, where baptism (or, more specifically, infant baptism) is concerned, this sacrament would accelerate the effects of
prevenient grace (or perhaps even justifying grace, depending upon
one's views or interpretation) so that the child and those acting on
behalf of the child are brought or elevated to a level of blessing
promised only to the faithful. More about that in a moment. For now,
however, it could be understood (though controversies *still* rage around
this issue) that infant baptism is an outward sign of an inward grace

at work in the child as confirmed by the faith of the church and those acting in behalf of the child, so that original sin does not make actual sin so devastating. Let's look closer.

Infant Baptism as Described by John Wesley

Although John Wesley makes no definitive statement about infant baptism that will yield consistently to all of his different comments on the subject (many of them seemingly contradictory), we can, for the sake of our purposes here, make some judgments that will assist us in pursuing a Wesleyan plan of salvation.

In his "A Treatise on Baptism," Wesley writes, "It [baptism] is the initiatory sacrament, which enters us into convenant with God. It was instituted by Christ, who alone has the power to institute a proper sacrament, a sign, seal, pledge, and means of grace, perpetually obligatory on all Christians."[4] Although this treatise is actually a reprint of a treatise published by his father Samuel (a high church sacramentalist) 50 years earlier, by publishing it under his own name, John is identifying with the doctrine as taught by the Church of England. On the surface it would appear (as the Church historian Albert Outler suggested) that Wesley is here trying to bolster the sagging conviction among many Methodists as to the validity of infant baptism as an experience of divine grace.[5]

Furthermore, if this treatise were our only source we could easily conclude that Wesley was a sacramentalist. That is, he was totally in line with the English reformers who taught that the new birth took place at the moment of infant baptism and made all subsequent appeals for a new birth, as an experience among baptized adults, redundant or unnecessary. Upon closer examination of his entire works, however, it is clear that although he agreed with the major tenets of this treatise in principle, there were certain areas where he differed substantially. For example, he appreciated the emphasis on the objectivity of grace. On the other hand, in so far as the treatise tended to undermine an evangelistic appeal for the new birth, he strongly objected.

Overall, three areas of concern seem to surface: 1. He wanted to counter the effects of the *enthusiasts* who believed that baptism was not important. 2. He wanted to warn those who relied totally upon baptism, as a past experience, for salvation. 3. He wanted to emphasize infant baptism as a means of accelerating the effects of prevenient grace.

United Methodist Bishop Ole Borgen writes,

> The theological (and practical) importance of the sacraments for Wesley lies in their function: Within the framework of the *ORDO SALUTIS* [the order of salvation], they function as (1) effective signs, (2) effective means of grace, and (3) effective pledges of glory to come, conjoined with the added aspect of sacrifice.[6]

Wesley is quick to add that there is no hint of magic here. "The grace does not spring merely ex opere operato: *It does not proceed from the mere elements, or the words spoken; but from the blessing of God.*

Although this strong statement seems to underscore the relevance of the sacraments for our "plan of salvation," Borgen seems to allow Wesley's reprint of his father's treatise to carry the day, as he then seems to conclude that John himself believed in baptismal regeneration (that is, one is actually "born again" at the time of infant baptism). Did Wesley believe in baptismal regeneration? Let's take a brief look at the treatise and then, from some comparisons from other sources, make our own decision.

After dispensing with opinions concerning the "method" (washing, dipping, or sprinkling) of baptism as unimportant, Wesley moves quickly to the benefits of baptism. Five are listed.

First, "the washing away the guilt of original sin, by the application of the merits of Christ's death."[7] Wesley adds that "this plainly includes infants; for they too die; therefore they have sinned: But not by actual sin; therefore, by original; else what need have they of the death of Christ?" In another setting Wesley is quick to add that there is no hint of magic here. "The grace does not spring merely *ex opere operato:* It does not proceed from the mere elements, or the words spoken; but from the blessing of God, in consequence of his promise to such as are qualified for it."[8] In other words, the grace is conveyed by virtue of God's faithfulness to a convenant promise in response to a convenant act.

Second, "By baptism we enter into convenant with God . . . ." The key here ties in with the Old Testament (or Old Covenant) understanding of circumcision. Wesley writes, "As circumcision was then the way of entering into this convenant, so baptism is now." Just as the Israelites convenanted with God to circumcise their infant boys on their eighth day, Christians are to baptize their infant babies. Wesley argues in part,

> Now, if infants were capable of being circumcised, notwithstanding that repentance and faith were to go before circumcision on grown persons, they are just as capable of being baptized; notwithstanding that repentance and faith are, in grown persons, to go before baptism.

Third, "By baptism we are admitted into the Church." Using the same argument as for the second benefit, Wesley writes, "The Jews were admitted into the Church by circumcision, so are the Christians by baptism."

Fourth, "By baptism, we who were 'by nature children of wrath' are made the children of God." Wesley adds, "And this regeneration which our Church in so many place ascribes to baptism is more than being admitted into the Church, . . . By water then, as a means, the water of baptism, we are regenerated or born again."

Finally, baptism makes us "heirs of the kingdom of heaven." From both of these last two benefits one can readily understand how Borgen could argue persuasively that Wesley was a sacramentalist. For example, it would appear that Wesley is making infant baptism concomitant with the new birth. We stated earlier that Wesley had three concerns. Having established the first, Wesley now addresses (although in a different setting) the second. In all of Wesley's remaining works, in spite of his views on the efficacy of infant baptism, he strongly counters

> *Just as the Israelites convenanted with God to circumcise their infant boys . . . Christians are to baptize their infant babies.*

those opinions that would seemingly undermine an evangelistic call for the new birth.

In his sermon on "The New Birth" he clearly states that the two do not always accompany one another.[9] He adds: "It is certain our Church *supposes* that all who are baptized in their infancy are at the same time born again."[10] Then without actually contradicting this (what Outler would have called a "mild allowance") he goes on to say, "But whatever be the case with infants, it is sure all of riper years who are baptized are not at the same time born again. 'The tree is known by its fruits.'"[11]

"But whatever be the case with infants, it is sure all of riper years who are baptized are not at the same time born again."

Lest you think Wesley has gone too soft, read this from his sermon "The Great Privilege of Those That Are Born of God":

> Lean no more on the staff of that broken reed, that ye *were* born again in baptism. Who denies that ye were then made children of God, and heirs of the Kingdom of heaven? But, notwithstanding this, ye are now children of the devil. Therefore ye must be born again.[12]

Without belaboring the various interpretations of infant baptism *ad nauseum*, let's see if we can clarify at least some of the issues before looking at possible scenarios illustrating Wesley's third concern (mentioned earlier), regarding the role of infant baptism in accelerating the effects of prevenient grace.

There is always the possibility that Wesley believed in both baptismal regeneration and the new birth as an experience of conversion. United Methodist Bishop William Cannon notes that Wesley spent a great deal of time pointing out that "baptism, the sign, is distinct from regeneration [or new birth], the thing signified." Wesley was attempting to demonstrate that baptism and the new birth can, but do not necessarily, occur with the outward sign of water baptism. Cannon argues that Wesley is trying to use accepted Church terminology while inserting his own interpretation of its meaning.[14]

Whatever the reasons for the apparent inconsistencies — whether it is a result of some misunderstanding in the meaning of terms, or of borrowing so much from his father's treatise, or of his desire to align himself with the Established Church — he eventually makes an honest effort to clear up the confusion in his sermon on "The New Birth." There he writes,

> Baptism is not the new birth: They are not one and the same thing. Many indeed seem to imagine that they are just the same; at least, they speak as if they thought so; but I do not know that this opinion is publicly avowed by any denomination of Christians whatever.[15]

If the issues are still unclear, let me attempt to simplify them by venturing a few possible scenarios.

Some Possible Scenarios in Understanding Wesley's Description of Infant Baptism

Although difficult to rationalize theologically (let alone biblically), one might surmise that Wesley is saying that we are perhaps justified with infant baptism but not born again. Although subsequent chapters will demonstrate that, for Wesley, justification and the new birth occur at the same time with adult believers (and this is no small point); where infant baptism is concerned this might be an exception.

Another possibility is that we are justified and even born again with infant baptism but that we lose "that washing of the Holy Ghost" (words used by Wesley to describe his own baptism) with actual sin, so that the new birth itself must be renewed. Wesley writes of infant baptism, "A principle of grace is infused, which will not be wholly taken away, unless we quench the Holy Spirit of God by long-continued wickedness."[16]

Still another possibility is that Wesley actually understood the "new birth" in two different and distinct ways. The link between the term regeneration and the new birth (used interchangeably) provides the clue. Before Wesley's "evangelical conversion" on Aldersgate Street he refers to the new birth only in the sacramental sense and with reference to baptism. After this time, however, he refers to the new birth in the evangelical sense and with reference to the change that takes place in persons at the point of a conscious change of the will towards God.

Holding to both these views might not play to the systematician, but it does explain the apparent inconsistencies. The common objection was: "I need not be born again: I was born again when I was baptized. What! Would you have me deny my baptism?" Wesley would respond that they had already denied their baptism: "Whenever you do any of the works of the devil, then you deny your baptism" and although you might have been born again in baptism, "still, you must be born again."

> *I wanted my children to cross the "river" at its narrowest and shallowest point.*

In the final analysis Wesley suggests that *normally* infants cannot be saved unless original sin be washed away by baptism. He then states that the unbaptized infant is not damned or sent to *Limbus Infantum*, as the Roman Catholics believe.[18] Baptism, therefore, although effective for washing away the guilt of *original* sin, is not absolutely necessary. In later chapters, however, we will observe that the new birth, among adults, *is* absolutely necessary for washing away the guilt of *actual* sin. More about that in a moment, but for now let's look briefly at some of the practical implications that speak to Wesley's third concern, that of grace accelerated.

The Doctrine Applied

I have heard it stated that the "greater the sinner, the greater the saint." Not true! The greater the sinner the more memory that lies just below the surface so that when our level of spirituality drops, it raises its ugly head to haunt us. The ideal is for the child to grow to maturity knowing nothing but "Jesus Christ and him crucified." I wanted my children to cross the "river" at its narrowest and shallowest point. I believe that infant baptism can assist the child in avoiding the deepest reaches of actual sin. Little wonder Wesley would write,

> If there are such inestimable benefits conferred in baptism, the washing away the guilt of original sin, the en-

grafting us into Christ, by making us members of his Church, and thereby giving us a right to all the blessings of the gospel; it follows, that infants may, yea, ought to be baptized, and that none ought to hinder them.[19]

Crisis conversions are wonderful. In most cases, however, the children who can avoid the "pit" (whose sins tend to "bore" us), make the strongest and most fruitful Christians. I wanted all of my children to thrill to the support of Christian community at an early age. Someone recently said to me that all she remembered of her early childhood church experiences was "dressing up, sitting still, keeping quiet, and making all sorts of things out of popsicle sticks." What a shame!

Infant baptism should be an important point in the process of salvation where children are, to use the words of Wesley, "mystically united to Christ, and made one with him." From this mystical union "proceeds the influence of his grace on those that are baptized; as from our union with the Church, a share in all its privileges, and in all the promises Christ has made to it."[20]

Recently, while on a train in northeastern China, I met four Russians on their way home to Vladivostok (the next stop on the line after my exit at Yanji). As we were getting acquainted the topic soon turned to religion. Each of them (although raised and educated in a State that is officially atheistic) had been baptized as infants at the insistance of their mothers. Not surprisingly, each of them had a residual curiosity about God. I sensed the Holy Spirit was continuing a work already begun. We talked half the night. I came away from that discussion determined to renew my own commitment to infant baptism.

Fortunately, many churches take the baptism of their children seriously. Here is a sample letter that a pastor friend of mine writes to all of the children baptized in his local church:

Dear _____

I wanted to write you a few words concerning something very special that happened in our church recently. It was the day of your baptism. The church was full, and everybody was eager for the big event. Your parents and your godparents were there, and took every minute of the service seriously.

During the service, your parents confessed their faith in Christ, and pledged to raise you according to the teachings of the Bible and in the fellowship of the church of Jesus Christ. Then we laid you, as it were, in the arms of God. We had good precedent on this from the Bible itself. The gospel of Matthew tells us how Jesus took time during one of the busiest days of His short ministry to take you "upon His lap" and to bless you. We sealed you in the name of the Father, Son and Holy Spirit, and asked God's Holy Spirit to come into your life and to cause you to hunger deeply for God's presence. We asked that you would be drawn close to God so that one day all we have believed and confessed for you might become your own faith and confession.

Undoubtedly, you will read these words many years hence, but I pray when you do, you will take to heart the fact that you are deeply loved by your parents and were genuinely blessed by the people of this church and its pastor. It is my prayer as the pastor of _____, that you will be raised happily and positively in the fellowship of God's people; that your experience of the things of God might be wholesome and rich; that becoming a Christian for you might be as natural as taking your first step. That's the way it ought to be when we finally come to believe for ourselves as Christians.

In the meantime, please know that your pastor has prayed for you and will continue to do so. I hope to get to know you better as you grow up and come to the day of your confirmation. I pray a blessing on your parents, who will probably have read this letter long before you see it. It was a great privilege to be able to serve your parents and you on the day you were baptized.

Your pastor,[21]

Review

Although the human condition is not changed with infant baptism (indeed, because of a lingering propensity to sin the individual inevitably sins by intention), I believe that prevenient grace, at work from conception, is accelerated with infant baptism (no small advantage) so that the effects of actual sin are not so devastating. If, however, we are justified with infant baptism (a possible Wesleyan scenario), we still need the new birth as the rite of baptism itself must then point to personal faith in Jesus Christ. The law is still a law of sin and death. The Spirit can act *upon* us, but where original sin still prevails, the Spirit cannot work *within* us.[23] Actual sin soon renews our condemnation. That unfortunate story must now be told.

Study Questions:

1. What is a sacrament?
2. How does infant baptism affect the life of the child?
3. What is the role of the parents?
4. What is the significance of "grace accelerated?"
5. What should children be taught about their baptism once they reach the age of accountability?

Notes

[1]These seven sacraments (adopted at the Council of Trent) were first set forth explicitly by Peter Lombard (in the twelfth century) who defined them as symbols and means of grace.

[2]Wesley's *Works*, Vol. 8, p. 31. Wesley is of course quoting from the "Articles of Religion" (article XIX) for the Church of England (italics mine).

[3]Wesley's *Standard Journal*, Curnock ed., Vol. 2, p. 315.

[4]Wesley's *Works*, Vol. 10, p. 188.

[5]Albert Outler, *John Wesley*, p. 318.

[6]Ole Borgen, *John Wesley on the Sacraments*, p. 47.

[7]Wesley's *Works*, Vol. 10, pp. 190ff. This is the same reference

for all five of the benefits listed below.

[8]Wesley's *Works*, Vol. 10, p. 149. This quotation is from a treatise entitled "Popery Calmly Considered."

[9]Wesley's *Works*, Vol. 6, p. 74.

[10]Wesley's *Works*, Vol. 6, p. 74 (italics mine).

[11]Wesley's *Works*, Vol. 6, p. 74. Cf. Fletcher, *Works*, Vol. 8, p. 384 where Fletcher exhorts: "Do not say, 'I was born again in baptism . . .'" Cf. also Vol. 8, p. 465 where Fletcher plainly states, "Water baptism alone will condemn you."

[12]Wesley's *Works*, Vol. 5, p. 222; cf. Vol. 6, pp. 75ff. It is interesting that Wesley was accused of preaching a redundant doctrine when he insisted that those baptized as infants be born again. This controversy closed the pulpits in the Church of England to his preaching for many years.

[13]Wesley's *Works*, Vol. 6, p. 73; cf. Cannon, *The Theology of John Wesley*, p. 126.

[14]Cannon, *The Theology of John Wesley*, p. 126.

[15]Wesley's *Works*, Vol. 6, p. 73.

[16]Wesley's *Works*, Vol. 10, p. 192.

[17]Wesley's *Works*, Vol. 6, pp. 75ff.

[18]Wesley's *Works*, Vol. 6, pp. 248f.

[19]Wesley's *Works*, Vol. 10, p. 198.

[20]Wesley's *Works*, Vol. 10, p. 191.

[21]This letter was sent to me by Robert Stamps, pastor of the Park Avenue United Methodist Church in Minneapolis, Minnesota.

[22]Wesley's *Works*, Vol. 5, p. 222. In my opinion the "Renewal of Baptismal Covenant" (e.g., see *The United Methodist Book of Worship*) is, and should be, a significant experience available, at least on a yearly basis, to the entire church.

[23]Wesley's *Works*, Vol. 5, p. 154.

Psalms 5:1-19   *Hebrews 12:5*
Romans 3:23; 8:1-4; *James 4:17*
14:22f

*Actual sin is our own
personal sin committed upon
the age of accountability
(when we consciously
understand the difference
between right and wrong)—a
willful disobedience. It is
important to remember that
for John Wesley one is not
condemned for original sin
alone but for original sin*
plus *actual sin.*

1. Wesley's overall doctrine of sin is discussed.

2. Actual sin is then related to the abuse of our power to obey (or disobey) God.

3. Actual sin must be acknowledged and confessed. We must then repent and believe the gospel lest we be hopelessly lost under the burden of the law of sin and death.

CHAPTER

5

The Law now brings its full force to bear. In our introductory chart we saw that before conversion the Law serves to condemn. Although it draws and convicts, it is

Actual Sin: The Age of Accountability

impossible, without grace, to fulfill the Law. The cause: a propensity to sin (the fruit of original sin) so that our fallen nature prevails. The effect: in spite of prevenient grace (and even with the possible advantage of infant baptism), "all sin and fall short of the glory of God" (Romans 3:23). Unfortunately, the story here is easily told. Let's look closer.

John Wesley's Doctrine of Sin

This is perhaps the area where Wesley has received the most criticism from those outside the Wesleyan tradition. In an attempt to explain *sinless perfection*, for example, "sinless" (a term he disliked) seems to be compatible with involuntary acts and emotions (due to ignorance and mistakes still needing an atonement) that most would consider sinful. Since perfection is a topic for a later chapter, we will allow just one quotation to illustrate this point before moving on to Wesley's broader understanding of the nature of sin itself.

> Now, mistakes, and whatever infirmities necessarily flow from the corruptible state of the body, are noway contrary to love; nor therefore, in the Scripture sense, sin.

> To explain myself a little farther on this head: (1.) Not only sin, properly so called, (that is, a voluntary transgression of a known law,) but sin, improperly so called, (that is, an involuntary transgression of a divine law, known or unknown,) needs the atoning blood. (2.) I believe there is no such perfection in this life as excludes these involuntary transgressions which I apprehend to be naturally consequent on the ignorance and mistakes inseparable from mortality.[1]

While statements like this might cause some to question his understanding of sin in general, few could challenge Wesley's commitment to overcoming the nature of sin.

The Nature of Sin

In his treatise, "On Original Sin," Wesley writes: "Sin is 'a transgression of the law;' of that law of God to which a rational creature is subject."[2] In another place he states that "nothing is sin, strickly speaking, but a voluntary transgression of a known law of God. Therefore, every voluntary breach of the law of love is sin; and nothing else, if we speak properly."[3]

"Every voluntary breach of the law of love is sin . . ."

Early in John's life his mother, Susanna, suggested that anything that diminished the relish for things spiritual was sin, and that this found its origin in self-will. Apparently taking her lead, Wesley himself writes that

> it would be endless to enumerate all the species of wickedness, whether in thought, word, or action, that now overspread the earth, in every nation, and city, and family.

They all centre in this, doing their own will, not the will of Him that made them.[4]

This is further explained in one of his sermons: "We have set up our idols in our hearts; and to these we bow down and worship them: We worship ourselves, when we pay that honour to ourselves which is due to God only."[5]

Closely connected to self-will is pride. Wesley adds,

Therefore all pride is idolatry; it is ascribing to ourselves what is due to God alone. And although pride was not made for man, yet where is the man that is born without it? But hereby we rob God of his unalienable right, and idolatrously usurp his glory.[6]

Behind self-will and pride the "sensual appetites" are soon to follow. Just as John's gospel records this warning from Jesus to some who brazenly claimed to be descendants of Abraham: "Everyone who sins is a slave to sin . . . [and] belongs to your father, the devil," so Wesley laments, "Sensual appetites, even those of the lowest kind, have, more or less, the dominion over him [humankind]. They lead him captive; they drag him to and fro, in spite of his boasted reason."[7]

Such is the nature of sin apart from the grace of God. It takes us captive. The law (at this point the "law of sin and death") serves only to highlight our misery. Listen to Wesley's description of his own struggle with sin prior to Aldersgate.

In this vile, abject state of bondage to sin, I was indeed fighting continually, but not conquering. I fell, and rose, and fell again. Sometimes I was overcome, and in heaviness: Sometimes I overcame, and was in joy. I had many sensible comforts; which are indeed no other than short anticipations of the life of faith. But I was still "under the law," not "under grace:" (The state most who are called Christians are content to live and die in:) For I was only striving with, not freed from, sin: Neither had I the witness of the Spirit with my spirit, and indeed could not; for I "sought it not by faith, but as it were by the works of the law.[8]

In a more general way Wesley describes this same struggle in all of us. Prevenient grace enlightens the law so that we fight against a "voluntary transgression" of it,

> but though he [humankind] strives with all his might, he cannot conquer: Sin is mightier than he. He would fain escape; but he is so fast in prison, that he cannot get forth. He resolves against sin, but yet sins on: He sees the snare, and abhors, and runs into it. So much does his boasted reason avail, — only to enhance his guilt, and increase his misery! Such is the freedom of the will; free only to evil; free to "drink in iniquity like water" to wander farther and farther from the living God, and do more "despite to the Spirit of grace!"[9]

Before picking up the discussion of actual sin at the age of accountability, some brief words need to be said about sin as relative and absolute; the sins of omission as well as commission; and finally the inward and outward natures of sin.

Sins of Omission as Well as Commission

A more subtle side of sin involves those areas of disobedience where we fail to fulfill our responsibilities as committed Christians.

How many of us are tempted to do or say nothing in the face of evil, especially when to do so places us in an awkward or difficult light?

Sin is more than doing wrong, disobeying a known law of God; it is also refusing to do what we know to be right, in some instances, simply doing nothing (James 4:17). How many of us are tempted to do or say nothing in the face of evil, especially when to do so places us in an awkward or difficult light? Again, if sin is the opposite of obedience to God (and that case could be easily made), then sin is more than doing wrong; it is failing to do right.

In 2 Kings 7, Samaria has been under siege by the Syrian army so that starvation is imminent for the entire city. Four lepers discover in the night that the enemy soldiers have abandoned their camp leaving all of their provisions behind.

Their first reaction is to gorge themselves without a thought for anyone else but then quickly conclude that "this isn't right. This is wonderful news, and we aren't sharing it with anyone! Even if we wait until morning, some terrible calamity will certainly fall upon us; come on, let's go back and tell the people" (2 Kings 7:9, *Living Bible*). I call that the "sin of silence."

Sin as Absolute and Relative

Certainly there are sins that are always sin under any circumstances. The "Ten Commandments" come immediately to mind. There are, however, certain acts (or non-acts) that are sin for some but not for others. This should be so obvious that it bears only a mention.

Romans 14, for example, speaks of abstaining from certain foods (which in themselves are harmless) so as not to be an offense to our sister or brother. Paul writes at the end of that chapter,

> *Certainly there are sins that are always sin under any circumstances.*

> "So whatever you believe about these things keep between yourself and God. Blessed is the man who does not condemn himself by what he approves. But the man who has doubts is condemned if he eats, because his eating is not from faith; and everything that does not come from faith is sin" (Rom. 14:22f).

Inward and Outward Sin

Wesley argues that sin is inward as well as outward. Since sin is rooted in *unbelief* (that is, refusing to believe that God deserves our highest loyalty; not letting God be God), sin becomes a disposition of the heart and will. Bishop Cannon writes that "the sins of the flesh are the children, not the parents, of pride; and self-love is the root, not the branch, of all evil."[10] Jesus, of course, insisted that,

> What comes out of a man is what makes him "unclean." For from within, out of men's hearts, come evil thoughts, sexual immorality, theft, murder, adultery, greed, malice, deceit, lewdness, envy, slander, arrogance and folly. All

these evils come from inside and make a man "unclean."[11]

For John Wesley, as well, the nature of sin involves a corruption from within that reveals itself in thought, word and deed. Just when this corruption cancels that "washing of the Holy Spirit" secured in baptism is the subject now to be addressed.

The Age of Accountability

At what age is one liable to judgment for sin? Some Wesleyans contend that *sin* (that propensity spoken of earlier) is imputed from birth, but not the *guilt* (spoken of here as that which is punishable). In other words, children sin by virtue of their inherited nature, but they are not held accountable until they sin willfully against any known law of God. Wesley himself is not altogether clear on this but he does make it clear that no one is punished or condemned for original sin alone, but for original sin *plus* actual sin.

Actual Sin Described

When children (or perhaps in some cases even adults) first abuse their power to obey God, actual sin is born.

Wesley implies that actual sin begins when the "use of reason" and "abuse" come together.[12] When children (or perhaps in some cases even adults) first abuse their power to obey God, actual sin is born. Although our propensity to sin causes reason and abuse to grow up together, liability to "all punishments in this world, and that which is to come" arises with intent. Again Wesley writes, "That all men are liable to these (punishments) for Adam's sin alone, I do not assert; but they are so, for their own outward and inward sins, which through their own fault, spring from the infection of their nature."[13]

Actual sin brings to bear the full penalty of the law. Prior to conversion this law is the law of sin and death. Adam's sin was characterized as thinking himself capable of life outside of God, to be a God unto himself. Satan (the Hebrew word for "accuser"), the ultimate source of all sin, suggested rebellion against God. By breaking fellowship with God, Adam violated all God's laws in a lump. Since sin involved God, actual sin for Adam was relational, it involved a conscious decision to disobey God.

Wesley talks about awakening the sleeper, those unaware that sin is first and foremost against God and causes alienation from God. In his sermon, "Awake, Thou that Sleepest," he writes: "Awake, thou everlasting spirit, out of thy dream of worldly happiness! Did not God create thee for himself? Then thou canst not rest till thou restest in him. Return, thou wanderer! Make haste. Eternity is at hand."[14] David writes in Psalm 51, "Have mercy on me, O God, ... For I know my transgressions, and my sin is always before me. Against you, you only, have I sinned and done what is evil in your sight."

> *"Awake, thou everlasting spirit, out of thy dream of worldly happiness! Did not God create thee for himself?"*

The law, once it is understood, brings sin to light. It makes sin (and guilt) real. Paul Tournier says that true guilt is "the genuine consciousness of having betrayed an authentic standard, it is a free judgment of the self by the self."[15] More about "guilt" in a moment, but for now our point is this: actual sin is the abuse of our freedom to choose by consciously disobeying God.

Real Guilt

Since some of us are uneasy with anything that is relative, there is a temptation to make all sin absolute and normative for the Church. In our discussion of sin as relative and absolute, we demonstrated briefly that (although there are absolutes) some things are sin for some but not for others. The failure to realize this can cause (for want of a better term) imaginary guilt. In other words, we (to use a Wesleyan phrase) cause people to grieve where God would not have them grieve. Let me explain further.

I have sometimes defined sin as anything that separates us from God, ourselves and those around us. I am then usually quick to add that if it is not separating us from God, ourselves and those around us, then we should stop worrying about it. There is enough real guilt in all of us so that we all need a savior; but there is imaginary guilt as well. We Christians have been known to "lay trips" on each other. That usually takes the form of some type of legalism. More about legalism in a moment, but for now we need to address the issue of guilt as real and imaginary (perhaps "neurotic" is a better word).

Scott Peck's book, *People of the Lie*, has convinced many of us that there is both real and neurotic guilt. Psychologists can help us with neurotic guilt (including the psychotic), but only God's grace can deal with the real (including the demonic). I have on occasion defined a Christian (in words close to those of Sam Shoemaker) as one who commits all that one knows of oneself to all that one knows of God. That speaks of two dimensions: the psychological and the theological. The psychological relates primarily to all that we know of ourselves. Each day we should find out more and more about ourselves so that we have more of ourselves to commit to God. The theological relates primarily to all that we know of God. Each day we should find out more and more about God so that we have more God to commit ourselves to. Let me illustrate.

> *We Christians have been known to "lay trips" on each other. That usually takes the form of some type of legalism.*

Sometimes when I attempt to pray, the "old history tapes" make so much noise that I simply cannot hear the voice of God. My mind is a whir. I must confess that I am sometimes asleep before I even start to pray. I become frustrated and guilt-ridden. If this continues for any length of time, I begin to lose an awareness of God in my life. I feel powerless. At this point I sometimes make an appointment with my friendly neighborhood Christian psychologist for the express purpose of lowering the volume on those old tapes so that I can once again hear the voice of God. I must never stop there, however. Psychology, although a valuable aid, in and of itself is a "rope of sand." We must then turn to God who alone can deal with the real guilt. Actual sin, although clouded by the neurotic, is still a reality.

Hebrews 12 speaks of a God who disciplines those whom God loves. God usually disciplines me through my conscience. If I am still sensitive enough to God's law so that I still feel guilty when I sin, that is not simply cause for shame, that is also cause for rejoicing because it means that God is still treating me as a son. We are encouraged not to "lose heart when God rebukes us" (Heb. 12:5).

God's discipline is clearly not punitive, but corrective. Problems, however, occur when we attempt to rationalize sin. One of the wonderful things that God did for me when I was converted nearly 30 years ago was

One of the wonderful things that God did for me when I was converted nearly 30 years ago was to spoil my ability to rationalize sin.

to spoil my ability to rationalize sin. I still sin (alas!), but I can no longer rationalize it. Sin and guilt are real, and God's forgiveness is available to any who repent and renew their faith and trust in Jesus Christ. Part II deals with this forgiveness (and the power "to go and sin no more") in great detail, but for now the reality of actual sin should be apparent. The following illustration should demonstrate this doctrine applied.

The Doctrine Applied

A few years ago I was introduced to a man just before I walked into a pulpit to preach. The pastor (a friend whose judgment I trust) described the man as the most spiritual person in the church. Quite frankly, the man looked spiritual to me. After I preached my sermon and gave the invitation, the first ones to the communion rail were this most spiritual person in the church and his wife. As I knelt to pray with them she leaned across the rail and whispered to me that I needed to pray for her. She was carrying a horrible secret. I, of course, prayed as best I knew how.

Then, as the wife returned to her pew, her husband, the most spiritual person in the church, remained behind. At that point he leaned across the rail and whispered, "You need to pray for me. I'm her secret. I'm an alcoholic, and I need will power."

I immediately responded, "Dear brother, you don't need will power; you need the power of the Holy Spirit." Let me explain.

I had just preached a sermon on Romans 8:1-4. In the introduction of this book I stated that if such a book could have a text, this was it. For sake of reference, let me give it to you again in its entirety.

> Therefore, there is now no condemnation for those who are in Christ Jesus, because through Christ Jesus the law of the Spirit of life set me free from the law of sin and death. For what the law was powerless to do in that it was weakened by the sinful nature, God did by sending his own Son in the likeness of sinful man to be a sin offering. And so he condemned sin in sinful man, in order that the righteous requirements of the law might be fully met in us, who do not live according to the sinful nature but according to the Spirit.

Question: Why would I deliver that good man back into the law of sin and death? The law of sin and death, the law without the Spirit, without the power nor the inclination to obey it, is legalism. Legalism dances to the tune of self-righteous obedience — self-induced will power. Most of us have struggled under the weight of legalism long enough.

> *... every time we repent and renew our faith and trust in Jesus Christ, we experience a fresh start, a new beginning.*

Legalism says that when we sin, repent and sin again, we are no longer capable of believing in the kind of a good God who would hear such feeble repentance. Our sin is compounded. It simply looms larger and larger. Have you any idea just how big a bottle is for an alcoholic? Try to stop sinning by trying not to sin. The sin will consume you. It's like trying not to think of something sweet when you're on a diet. You'll think of nothing *but* sweets.

Grace, on the other hand, redirects our attention. Grace taps the infinite reservoir of God's Holy Spirit. Grace says that when we sin, repent and sin again, we are still capable of believing in the kind of a good God who hears even our feeble repentance, so that every time we repent and renew our faith and trust in Jesus Christ, we experience a fresh start, a new beginning. The law of the Spirit of life — the law transformed by the power of God — is available so that the next time we are tempted our first inclination is to resist it. It will actually be easier to resist the temptation than to yield to it.

Many of us do not understand that power available "in Christ." We simply continue to sin out of habit. It is the right time of day, or the right time of the month. We do not even want to sin. The point is, we do not have to. Legalism relates to what we *cannot* do. Grace relates to what God *can* do. Would you like some of that? This is the story now to be told.

Review

Sin has been defined as disobeying a known law of God. Susanna Wesley defined it as anything that diminishes the appetite for things spiritual. I define it as anything that separates us from God, from ourselves or from those around us.

Again, actual sin is the abuse of our freedom to choose by consciously disobeying God. Just as it is important to understand in order to disobey, it is equally important to understand in order to remedy the alienation caused by disobedience.

Sin is first against God. Wesley would awaken the sleeper who failed to comprehend the seriousness of the problem. God desires reconciliation and makes loving provision through repentance and faith in the gift of God's son Jesus Christ.

Real guilt leads to repentance (introduced in our next chapter), or grief over an awareness of actual sin (which has alienated us from the One who loves us most), and must then lead to faith which, according to Wesley, is God's gift of grace by the operation of the Holy Spirit.[16]

This concludes Part I, "The Law of Sin and Death." Although created in the image of God (original righteousness), original sin prevails in spite of prevenient grace and even the particular advantage of infant baptism. Without the work of grace available through Jesus Christ, this is our lot. The law of sin and death rules. That is the bad news. Now that we have seen what the Enemy can do, let's see what God can do. Remember the "most spiritual person in the church"? The rest of his story will unfold in the chapters to follow.

Study Questions:

1. What is actual sin?
2. Can you think of sins of omission as well as sins of commission?
3. What kinds of sins are "absolute?" What kinds might be considered "relative?"
4. What is the significance of the "age of accountability?"
5. What is the difference between "real" and "neurotic" guilt?

Notes

[1]Wesley's *Works*, Vol. 11, p. 396.

[2]Wesley's *Works*, Vol. 9, p. 409.

[3]Wesley's *Works*, Vol. 12, p. 394.

[4]Wesley's *Works*, Vol. 7, pp. 338f.

[5]Wesley's *Works*, Vol. 6, p. 60.

[6]Wesley's *Works*, Vol. 6, p. 60.

[7]Wesley's *Works*, Vol. 6, p. 61; cf. John 8:34, 44.

[8]Wesley's *Works*, Vol. 1, p. 101.

[9]Wesley's *Works*, Vol. 5, p. 104.

[10]William Cannon, *The Theology of John Wesley*, p. 193.

[11]Mark 7:20-23.

[12]Wesley's *Works*, Vol. 9, p. 295.

[13]Wesley's *Works*, Vol. 9, p. 286.

[14]Wesley's *Works*, Vol. 5, p. 29.

[15]Paul Tournier, *Guilt and Grace*, p. 64 (Hodder and Stoughton, 1962).

[16]Wesley's *Works*, Vol. 5, p. 29.

PART II:
GRACE, THE POWER OF THE HOLY SPIRIT

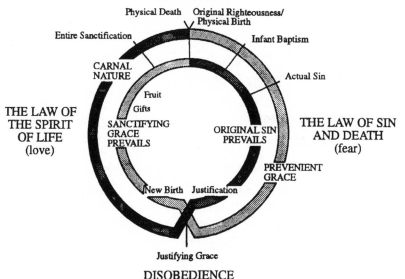

Justifying grace is the work of the Holy Spirit at the moment of conversion whereby the process *of moving toward disobedience is stopped and the* process *of moving back toward obedience is* begun. *Note, this does not imply perfection. The plunge toward a life of disobedience has simply been reversed.*

1. Prevenient grace (for those with ears to hear) leads to repentance and faith.
2. Faith then releases the indwelling power of the Holy Spirit.
3. Justifying grace then puts us right with God.

CHAPTER

6

In our introductory diagram (p. 63), we now find ourselves at the point of conversion signified there by justifying grace leading to justification and the new birth.

Justifying Grace: the Spirit In You

Since the next two chapters describe justification and the new birth in some detail, here we will address the overall concept of justifying grace.

Within the theological schema of good news (original righteousness)/bad news (original sin)/good news (God in Christ reconciling and restoring us to our original righteousness), we are now as far from obedience (and as close to disobedience) as we get. Although we were created in the image of God (the original good news), we are now "very far gone from original righteousness" (the bad news).

Ultimately, the law of sin and death has served only to frustrate and condemn. Original sin has prevailed. Sin has reigned. Although prevenient grace has prevented us from moving so far toward disobedience that when we finally understand the claims of the gospel upon our lives, we are guaranteed the freedom to say yes; so far, the "yes" has eluded us. Things are about to turn around.

The story of this "turn around" can be captured by the Scripture verses: "By grace you have been saved, through faith — and this is not from yourselves, it is the gift of God — not by works, so that no one can boast" (Ephesians 2:8-9). Let's break this down. Wesley follows up prevenient grace with convincing grace/repentance, faith and justifying grace. We will take these one at a time.

Convincing Grace/Repentance

First of all, it might be well to remember our association of grace with the work of the Holy Spirit. Grace is grace. The various adjectives qualifying grace simply describe the work of the self-same Spirit at various points along the continuum. Prevenient grace identifies the work of the Spirit between conception and conversion. Included in that, convincing grace describes the work of the Spirit just prior to salvation. Wesley writes,

> Salvation begins with what is usually termed (and very properly) *preventing* [or prevenient] grace; . . . Salvation is carried on by *convincing grace*, usually in Scripture termed *repentance*; which brings a larger measure of self-knowledge, and a farther deliverance from the heart of stone. Afterwards we experience the proper Christian salvation; whereby, "through grace," we "are saved by faith"; consisting of those two grand branches, justification and sanctification . . . All experience, as well as Scripture, show this salvation to be both instantaneous and gradual.[1]

The term "gradual" is important. Although many rightly believe that salvation is an experience culminating in a moment, a gradual process precedes all such experience. Prior to salvation the Holy Spirit serves not only to "woo" or draw but to convince and convict of sin. This awakening to sin, which leads to repentance, is related to a broader term, "conversion."

In his book *Conversion*, Erik Routley states that in the Bible "to convert" means "to turn."[2] In Acts 3:19, for example, the implication is "Stop! You are moving in the wrong direction."[3] For Wesley (as we shall soon see) that would suggest only half the story. Before turning to Wesley himself, however (since Wesley insisted that he was *homo unius libri*, a "man of one book," namely the Bible), it would serve us well to begin with our own brief examination of the biblical terms for conversion.

Although the biblical words relating to conversion are rarely translated as such, the roots of the various terms are found throughout the Old and New Testaments.[4] George Morris, in his book, *The Mystery and Meaning of Christian Conversion*, provides a fairly extensive study of these words related to the concept of conversion.[5]

Morris' chapter, "The Biblical Meaning of Conversion," begins with the Latin *conversus* (and its past participle, *convertere*), meaning to turn around, to revolve, to reverse or to change direction. Both the Hebrew and Greek words translated conversion have much the same meaning. Since *conversus* is obviously related to the New Testament understanding of repentance, it is not surprising to find that the Hebrew word *shûbh* (used over a thousand times in the Old Testament), meaning "to return" or "turn back," is translated in the New Testament by the Greek word *metanoeó*, meaning "to repent" or "to change one's mind." It should also be no surprise that *metanoeó* can also be translated "to be converted." These translations are significant in that they establish the relationship between repentance and the more comprehensive implications of conversion.

Another related term, *epistrephó*, meaning "to turn" or "return," can also be translated "to be converted." When *metanoeó* and *epistrephó* appear together (Luke 17:4; Acts 3:19; 26:18-20, e.g.) the full meaning of conversion becomes more and more apparent. Again, Acts 3:19, "Repent (*metanoeó*) then and turn (*epistrephó*) to God," demonstrates this. Although some argue (albeit inconclusively, in my opinion) that both terms should be translated "conversion," it seems more reasonable to me to acknowledge that the two terms together demonstrate the gradual and the instantaneous aspects of conversion. Convincing grace brings repentance leading to the point of faith. The act of faith should now attract our full attention.

Faith Is the Key

In the text previously cited, "By grace you have been saved through faith," the phrase "by grace" refers to the gradual work of the Spirit acting preveniently and convincingly, leading to an awareness of sin and the need for repentance. "Through faith" refers to what I call the "I give up." Let's allow Wesley to establish the context.

Wesley tells us that he preached basically three kinds of sermons. To the unawakened (those not yet convicted of sin), he spoke mainly of death and hell (since to speak to the unawakened of "justification" would be like talking Greek). To those awakened (but not yet converted), he spoke mainly of faith. To those converted, he spoke mainly of perfection or entire sanctification.

For a moment let's focus at the point of his evangelistic appeal — to those awakened. Faith is the key. Wesley goes to great lengths to define it. He tells us what it is not. It is not that faith of a heathen, nor of a devil, nor even that of the apostles while Christ remained in the flesh.[6] He tells us what it is. It is, in a general sense,

> a divine supernatural, *evidence* or *conviction*, "of things not seen," not discoverable by our bodily senses, as being either past, future, or spiritual.

> Justifying faith implies, not only a divine evidence or conviction that "God was in Christ, reconciling the world unto himself"; but a sure trust and confidence that Christ died for *my* sins, that He loved *me* and gave Himself for *me*.[7]

The passage following this statement provides a further key. There he speaks of *repentance*. Wesley's evangelistic thrust insisted that faith build upon a firm foundation. The repentance that led to faith was for Wesley what I have already referred to as the "I give up."

I Give Up

It is my conviction that Wesley's "instantaneous" conversion experience took 13 years to manifest itself fully. The reason for the delay was that it took considerable effort to divest himself of the bankruptcy of his own works-righteousness. Wesley, just prior to Aldersgate, included in his journal these words from a letter written to his brother Charles from one of the early Methodists, John Gambold, prefacing them with the statement that he found them "so true." Gambold writes,

> The doctrine of faith is a downright robber. It takes away

all this wealth, and only tells us it is deposited for us with somebody else, upon whose bounty we must live like mere beggars. Indeed, they are truly beggars, vile and filthy sinners till very lately, many stoop to live in this dependent condition: It suits them well enough. But they who have long distinguished themselves from the herd of vicious wretches, or have even gone beyond moral men; for them to be told that they are either not so well, but the same needy, impotent, insignificant vessels of mercy with the others: This is more shocking to reason than transubstantiation.[8]

Even before leaving for Georgia, Wesley sensed that something was amiss. At that point he attempted to exchange the outward works of "visiting the sick or clothing the naked" for the inward works of a pursuit of holiness, "or a union of the soul with God." He comments later that "in this refined way of trusting to my own works and my own righteousness (so zealously inculcated by the mystic writers), I dragged on heavily, finding no comfort or help therein."[9]

At long last Wesley resolved to seek salvation through faith by first of all "absolutely renouncing all dependence, in whole or in part, upon *my own* works or righteousness; on

> *Even before leaving for Georgia, Wesley sensed that something was amiss.*

which I had really grounded my hope of salvation, though I knew it not, from my youth up."[10] This was the point at which Wesley "gave up." *His besetting sin was a misplaced trust!* He repented. He *gave up* his faith in his own self-righteousness and determined to trust Christ alone as his "sole justification, sanctification, and redemption." Aldersgate and his "evangelical" conversion followed shortly thereafter.

For the rest of Wesley's life, this "I give up," this (to use the words of Thomas á Kempis) "following naked the naked Jesus" became the spearhead for his evangelistic appeal. His watchwords included such warnings as: Do not trust that staff of a broken reed, believing solely in your infant baptism for salvation. Do not trust anyone or anything else for salvation apart from Christ. He writes,

As 'there is no other name given under heaven,' than that of Jesus of Nazareth, no other merit whereby a condemned sinner can ever be saved from the guilt of sin; so there is no other way of obtaining a share in His merit, than by faith in His name.[11]

Whenever I insist on the uniqueness of our faith in Christ alone for salvation some of my students respond, "How can you be so narrow-minded?" My reply?

"My believing in the uniqueness of our faith in Jesus Christ does not necessarily make me right, but it sure makes me an evangelist." Truth does not change to accommodate what I believe truth to be. If God is a triangle and I believe God is a circle, God does not become a circle to accommodate who or what I believe God to be. God remains a triangle just as truth remains truth, regardless of who or what I believe God or truth to be.

Having said that, however, I am absolutely committed to what I believe. I am not saying that I am right and the rest of the world is wrong. I *am* saying that I believe I am right. Furthermore, if anyone could prove that I am wrong or, for that matter, that Jesus Christ is not who he says he is, as I understand him to be portrayed in the Scriptures, my life would have no more meaning and purpose. That is just how much of me is at stake. If you have found a better way, I hope that you love me enough to let me in on your secret. In the meantime, I have searched the world over and can find none other. Let me explain further.

> *"My believing in the uniqueness of our faith in Jesus Christ does not necessarily make me right, but it sure makes me an evangelist."*

I recently returned from an extended trek throughout China, southeast Asia, India, the Middle East, North Africa and Eastern Europe. One of my primary objectives was to sense what God is doing in third world countries where the light of Christ does not shine so brightly. I was also looking for cross-cultural common denominators, concepts (or even ideologies) that communicate with more or less equal effectiveness across all cultural boundaries. I'll cite just three examples of what I found.

Apparently the music of Madonna is universal. I heard her music playing everywhere. Second, basketball is apparently universal. I saw basketball courts everywhere. (The only electric light I saw in one village was over a basketball hoop, and several local boys played nearly all night.) Third, an "oughtness" (a moral, cultural or even religious law) is also universal. Furthermore, in every culture, anyone who is *serious* about knowing God eventually becomes frustrated with his or her own inability to "measure up" to whatever "law" and is ripe for the good news that grace (the power of the Holy Spirit to obey such a law) is available through faith in Jesus Christ. In fact, I submit that Jesus Christ is even more cross-cultural than basketball or the music of Madonna. I know that

> *In every culture, anyone who is serious about knowing God eventually becomes frustrated with his or her own inability to "measure up"*

sounds like bias, and grumble if you must, but that is my own observation after interview upon interview. Let me explain further.

The Point of Least Resistance

I have always thought it interesting that the Greek word *pneuma* (spirit) translates the Hebrew word *ruach* (wind) in the Greek translation of the Hebrew Scriptures. Wind equals spirit and spirit equals wind. That is no accidental metaphor. Most of us know that wind blows from high pressure to low pressure, to the point of least resistance. One does not have to convince wind to blow from high pressure to low pressure; that is what wind does. Low pressure cells over bodies of water can attract wind at more than 200 miles per hour. Likewise, the Holy Spirit (in this instance, prevenient and justifying grace) moves from high pressure to low pressure, to the point of least resistance, to the "I give up."

Similarly, one does not have to convince the Holy Spirit to move from high pressure to low pressure; that is what the Spirit does. Salvation (and basic spirituality for that matter) is not so much "grunt and groan" as *repent and believe*. That is precisely why so much is at stake.

Faith in Christ alone — the "yes," the "I give up on my own self-righteousness and place my faith and trust in the righteousness of Christ" — creates low pressure. Again, the Holy Spirit no longer woos, but rushes to the very core of our being, creating and recreating after the mind of Christ. More of the theology behind this will be discussed in the next two chapters, but for now (recalling our introductory chart again), it is important to realize that the Holy Spirit as justifying grace moves inside the circle to continue as sanctifying grace. In that same moment sin moves outside the circle (though sin remains, it no longer reigns) and continues as the carnal nature. Before moving on to a more general discussion of justifying grace, allow an old evangelist a word of exhortation. You can take it.

People the world over are being drawn by the Spirit of God. The prevenient grace of God is at work all around us. Yet too many people, like Wesley, are weary of the bankruptcy of their own self-sufficiency. They are restless and uneasy. They cannot change their own lives. They cannot turn around. Their marriages are failing at an alarming rate. Most do not like doing what they do. Those with jobs can look forward to a two-day weekend, or a two-week vacation, or, for the less fortunate, a solid piece of meat or a good education for the eldest child, but little more. Many are discontent with a form of godliness which denies the power to pull it off. They are weary of the law without strength or inclination to obey. Do not despair, however, here is good news!

Although 1 John 5:19 says "that the whole world is under the control of the evil one," 1 John also says that God's "commands are not burdensome, for everyone born of God overcomes the world. This is the victory that has overcome the world, even our faith. Who is it that overcomes the world? Only he who believes that Jesus is the Son of God" (vv. 3-5). "Overcoming," perhaps John's favorite word (cf. Revelation, chapters 2-3), establishes the urgency of the gospel. Want to survive? Repent and believe the gospel!

Justifying Grace

Justifying grace describes the work of the Holy Spirit at the moment of conversion. At this point, it is important to give a more general description of the miracle that occurs in this moment.

Law and Grace

Law and grace are frequently pitted one against the other. That is a mistake. Both must be seen in tandem to maintain the integrity of the gospel. More about that later, but for now, Law, from the Old Testament perspective, makes one aware of sin (Rom. 3:20). In the New Testament, grace, the work of the Spirit, leads one to Christ (John 15:26).

Some believe that Jews begin and end with the Old Testament law and that Christians begin and end with New Testament grace. Not true! Both Jews and Christians begin with the law. Jews interpret the Old Testament law in light of the Mishnah and the Talmud. Christians interpret the Old Testament law in light of the New Testament grace revealed in Jesus Christ. Jesus Christ is our Mishnah and our Talmud.

Law without grace is a law of sin and death. Acts 15:10 asks, "Why do you try to test God by putting on the necks of the disciples [Gentile Christians] a yoke that neither we [Jews] nor our Fathers have been able to bear?" Paul writes, "The law was put in charge to lead us to Christ, . . . so that by faith we might receive the promise of the Spirit" (Gal. 3:14, 34). Law empowered by grace is the law of the Spirit of life. Someone has said that "grace is when you get what you *need*, not what you want or deserve."

It has already been demonstrated that Paul is not contrasting grace with law, but grace with the works of the law. Jesus insists, "Do you think that I have come to abolish the Law or the Prophets; I have not come to abolish them but to fulfill them" (Mt. 5:17). In subsequent chapters "grace fulfilling the law" will be a repeated theme.

Swoosh!

Imagine cause and effect. If our "initiative" (to God's initiative) is faith, then God's response is the power of the Holy Spirit rushing to the very core of our being — swoosh. "Swoosh," however, is *fact*, not *feeling*. Do not look for some emotional charge. Furthermore, do not be misled by the terms "cause and effect." The cause as well as the effect is enabled by God's grace.

In Wesley's "Predestination Calmly Considered," someone objects, "If man has any free will, then God cannot have the whole glory of his salvation." Wesley responds,

What do you mean by God's "having the whole glory?" Do you mean, "His doing the whole work, without any concurrence on man's part?" If so, your assertion is, "If man do at all 'work together with God,' in 'working out his own salvation,' then God does not do the whole work, without man's 'working together with Him.'" Most true, most sure: But cannot you see, how God nevertheless may have all the glory? Why, the very power to "work together with Him" was from God. Therefore to Him is all the glory . . . . We allow, it is the work of God alone to justify, to sanctify, and to glorify; which three comprehend the whole of salvation.[12]

Justifying grace is God's faithful response to our act of faith which is itself the work of God's grace. "Grace upon grace" is a worthy saying. Justifying grace is preceded by grace (God's *first* loving us) and followed by grace. It is time now to take a closer look at the experience itself established by grace.

Review

Prevenient grace prepares us for repentance and belief. Our "yes" then creates low pressure so that the Holy Spirit no longer woos, but rushes to the very core of our being, creating and recreating after the mind of Christ. Wesley at Aldersgate "gave up" his own self-righteousness for

a full reliance on the blood of Christ; a trust in the merits of his life, death, and resurrection; a recumbency upon him as our atonement and our life, *as given for us*, and *living in us*; and, in consequence hereof, a closing with him and cleaving to him, as our "wisdom, righteousness, sanctification, and redemption," or, in a word, our salvation.[13]

Wesley experienced justifying grace. Remember "the most spiritual person in the church" introduced at the end of our last chapter? When he returned to his pew his wife hardly recognized him. He has been sober ever since for he, too, had experienced justifying grace, a conversion which Wesley describes in terms of justification and new birth.

Study Questions:

1. What is justifying grace?
2. What are the gradual and the instantaneous aspects of conversion?
3. How does "faith" relate to the "I give up?"
4. What is the significance of "high pressure, low pressure?"
5. What is the role of Jesus Christ in all of this?

Notes

[1]Wesley's *Works*, Vol. 6, p. 509.

[2]Erik Routley, *Conversion*, p. 1.

[3]Erik Routley, *Conversion*, p. 1.

[4]Wesley writes that "'conversion' is a term which I rarely use, because it rarely occurs in the New Testament" (Wesley's *Works*, Vol. 9, p. 8); but then makes over one hundred references to "conversion" throughout his works. Proof again that Wesley was no "martyr to the bugbear of consistency."

[5]George Morris, *The Mystery and Meaning of Christian Conversion*, pp. 32-41.

[6]Wesley's *Works*, Vol. 5, pp. 8f.

[7]Wesley's *Works*, Vol. 5, pp. 60f.

[8]Wesley's *Works*, Vol. 1, p. 96.

[9]Wesley's *Works*, Vol. 1, p. 100.

[10]Wesley's *Works*, Vol. 1, p. 102.

[11]Wesley's *Works*, Vol. 5, pp. 209f.

[12]Wesley's *Works*, Vol. 10, p. 230.

[13]Wesley's *Works*, Vol. 5, p. 9.

Leviticus 1:4-9;   *Hebrews 9:1-10:18*
16:1-34; 17:11

Justification is the side of conversion that denotes a turning from sin *— what God does* for *us in Jesus Christ. It is an imputed righteousness or that which is attributed to us by virtue of our faith in Christ — a relative change.*

1. Justification turns us *from* sin.
2. The old covenant is replaced by a new covenant so that sin is no longer "covered over" but "rooted out" so that our sins are forgiven.
3. The righteousness of Jesus Christ is then attributed to believers by virtue of their faith in him.

CHAPTER

7

It is now time to explain the conversion that takes place as a result of justifying grace. For Wesley, conversion refers both to justification and to the new birth as

Justification: the Forgiveness of Sins

two aspects of one experience happening at the same point in time (with the possible exception of infant baptism, see Chapter 4). Wesley writes,

But though it be allowed, that justification and the new birth are, in point of time, inseparable from each other, yet are they easily distinguished, as being not the same, but things of a widely different nature. Justification implies only a relative, the new birth a real, change. God in justifying us does something *for* us; in begetting us again, he does the work *in* us. The former changes our outward relation to God, so that of enemies we become children; by the latter our inmost souls are changed, so that of sinners we become saints. The one restores us to the favor, the other to the image, of God. The one is the taking away the guilt, the other the taking away of the power, of sin: So that, although they are joined together in point of time, yet are they of wholly distinct natures.[1]

Again, theology gets us in touch with the mechanics of salvation. It may not be necessary to understand just what makes an automobile run in order to drive it, but if something goes wrong, it is essential to have some knowledge if we are to diagnose the problem and put it right.

Remember, bad theology can deliver us into bondage, seemingly left alone on some abandoned road to fend for ourselves. Good theology can set the captive free, empowering us to continue our journey with faith and hope. A healthy understanding of what puts us right with God and keeps us right with God can save us much time and energy and prevent costly repairs. With that in mind, we will look first of all at *justification* as the first aspect or phase of a two-sided conversion. Let's examine justification as the *terminus-a-quo* (turning from sin as exposed by the law of sin and death); as objective/forensic or legal; as God *for* us (the work of God in Jesus Christ); and as imputed righteousness, a relative change, entitling us to heaven. The following diagram might assist us in anticipating these two chapters.

The Two Sides of Conversion

"SAVED FROM" *Justification*	"SAVED INTO" *New Birth*
• turning *from* sin exposed by the law of sin and death, the *terminus-a-quo*, fear rules.	• turning to righteousness by the law of the Spirit of life, the *terminus-ad-quem*, love rules.
• objective/forensic (legal).	• subjective/personal.
• God *for* us (the work of God in Christ).	• God *in* us (the work of the Holy Spirit), the *beginning* of:
• imputed righteousness.	• imparted righteousness
• relative change	• a real change.
• entitled to heaven.	• qualified for heaven.

"it is for freedom that we've been set free"

94

Justification as the Turning from Sin

Someone has said that an army must sometimes retreat before it can advance. Although justification as the turning from sin (the *terminus-a-quo*) is not a retreat as such, it does lead us to acknowledge our sin, abhor it and then to repent. In my own walk with God, one of my greatest fears is that I might lose my sensitivity to sin. The words to Charles Wesley's hymn, "I Want a Principle Within," have convicted me time and again.

> I want a principle within of watchful, godly fear,
> a sensibility of sin, a pain to feel it near.
> I want the first approach to feel
> of pride or wrong desire,
> to catch the wandering of my will,
> and quench the kindling fire.

Furthermore, much of my own God-given "innate" spirituality depends upon my remaining sensitive to those things that separate, but that is the story for another chapter. For now, be advised; to be justified is to turn one's back on an old way of life. Sin is a lie, the great deceiver. It promises that which it can never ultimately produce, joy. The Psalmists frequently place joy in God far above temporal "happiness."

> Therefore my heart is glad and my tongue rejoices;
> my body also will rest secure,
> because you will not abandon me to the grave,
> nor will you let your Holy One see decay.
> You have made known to me the path of life;
> you will find me with joy in your presence,
> with eternal pleasures at your right hand (Ps. 16:9-11).

God is not some cosmic killjoy. God is against sin because sin does not work. Jumping off some high pinnacle does not break the law of gravity; the law of gravity breaks us. Turning from the law of sin and death acknowledges the inability of the law (in and of itself) to produce righteousness. God alone affects that kind of change. Let's look closer.

Justification As Objective/Forensic (legal)

Although terms such as forensic and legal tend to dehumanize when speaking of what God has done for us in Jesus Christ, it is important to realize that within the "covenant of promise" established with Abraham, God's own justice (as well as God's mercy) required a sacrifice for sin. Justification, therefore, looks at conversion more objectively, in the forensic or legal sense of "being put right with God" (the literal translation of *dikaios*, the Greek word for justification).

> *The Old Testament sacrifice served only to "cover over" (to propitiate) sin. It was like sweeping sin under the rug.*

I have sometimes argued (perhaps foolishly) that if the world would grant me the necessity of a sacrifice for sin (though God's Word states it plainly, Hebrews 9:22, e.g.), I could reason my way to faith in Christ. Leviticus 16 establishes the background. There the sacrifices on the "Day of Atonement" are described as the means for receiving the forgiveness of sins for the nation as well as the individual. Sacrifice, throughout the Bible, is depicted as God's way of underscoring the seriousness of sin (Leviticus 1:4-9). The blood of an innocent animal (blood being the symbol of life, cf. Leviticus 17:11) was substituted for the guilt of the people.

In the Old Testament, however, the sacrifice of animals was merely a shadowy precursor for what God would do perfectly in Jesus Christ. The Old Testament sacrifice served only to "cover over" (to propitiate) sin. It was like sweeping sin under the rug. It had to be repeated year after year. Hebrews 10:1 speaks of a "shadow" (perhaps reminiscent of Plato's "cave"), not the "realities themselves." In the New Testament this would all change.

God no doubt wearied of sacrifices that did not produce obedience (1 Samuel 15:22f, cf. Hebrews 10:5f). Jeremiah 31:31, serving as pivot between old and new, speaks of a "new covenant." Here the sacrifice of God's own Son would be made once for all as sin was no longer simply covered over but rooted out (expiated).[2] The new covenant was a tabernacle not made with hands, eternal in the heavens. Hebrews 9:23-24 reads,

It was necessary, then, for the copies of the heavenly things to be purified with these sacrifices, but the heavenly things themselves with better sacrifices than these. For Christ did not enter a man-made sanctuary that was only a copy of the true one; he entered heaven itself, now to appear for us in God's presence.

Let me illustrate the importance of this point. Imagine two Israelite men approaching the temple for sacrifice under the old covenant. One is wealthy and leads a prime heifer. The other is poor and carries a small bird. Although it might not be the nature of the one who is wealthy to be prideful, as he approaches the altar he catches sight of the one with the bird and, before he can catch himself, finds himself swelling with a sense of importance as if to say, "I have a heifer while my friend has only a bird. Surely I am more spiritual". The result was that the very thing that God instituted to draw the nation together was dividing the body.

The solution to this problem was revealed in Jesus Christ. In effect God is saying, "I will establish a new covenant with my people. I will provide the sacrifice myself. Since they have rejected my prophets, I will place my own Son upon a cross and *create level ground beneath it.*" No more heifer and no more bird. Under the new covenant we all approach God by the same means, by placing our faith and trust in God's provision for the forgiveness of our sins. In fact, one of the reasons that I am a Christian is that once the importance of the sacrifice was clear in my own mind, I searched the world over for someone (or even something) sufficient to fulfill the nature of the new covenant (i.e., "perfect in every way"), and I could only find Him on a Cross. Let's look even closer.

Justification as God FOR Us
(The Work of Jesus Christ)

Wesley writes at great length about the work God does *for* us at the moment of justification. If the forensic side of justification satisfies God's justice in light of the significance and necessity of a sacrifice for sin, then what God does *for* us in Jesus Christ speaks of God's mercy. In his sermon, "Justification by Faith," Wesley states,

"God so loved the world, that he gave his only-begotten Son, to the end we might not perish, but have everlasting life." In the fulness of time he was made Man, another common Head of mankind, a second general Parent and Representative of the whole human race. And as such it was that "he bore our griefs," "the Lord laying upon him the iniquities of us all." Then was he "wounded for our transgressions, and bruised for our iniquities." "He made his soul an offering for sin": He poured out his blood for the transgressors: He "bare our sins in his own body on the tree," that by his stripes we might be healed: And by that one oblation of himself, once offered, he hath redeemed me and all mankind; having thereby "made a full, perfect, and sufficient sacrifice and satisfaction for the sins of the whole world."[3]

The powerful image of "being washed in the blood" apparently makes some uneasy, but I refuse to give it up.

God's mercy, like God's justice, is mediated through faith in the death (and resurrection) of God's Son Jesus Christ and is applied by grace as the work of God's Holy Spirit. John Wesley was once asked, "For whose sake, or by whose merit, do you expect to enter into the glory of God?"

Wesley responded, "I answer, without the least hesitation, For the sake of Jesus Christ the Righteous. It is through his merits alone that all believers are saved; that is, justified — saved from the guilt, sanctified — saved from the nature, of sin, and glorified — taken into heaven."[4]

Wesley also reminds us that justification is "pardon, the forgiveness of sins."[5] Our sins have been blotted out. The powerful image of "being washed in the blood" apparently makes some uneasy, but I refuse to give it up. I once preached for several weeks in a church in Singapore that had a blood-red ceiling symbolizing the shed blood of Jesus. Every time I looked at that ceiling I was reminded afresh of just what God has done for us. Images like that serve as a memory jog.

One of the reasons I have such appreciation for the "Holy Land" is that it shouts its own history. The children of Israel were always erecting piles of stone to remind them of God's faithfulness. The celebration of the Lord's Supper, of course, is an even more significant "remembrance." As Christians partake of the elements, that act of remembrance accelerates the work of the Holy Spirit so that the community is empowered in a special way to do God's will. Our justification implies a covering. Just as the innocence of the animal sacrificed was attributed to the believer in the old covenant, the righteousness of Jesus Christ is attributed to Christians. Theologians sometimes refer to this "covering" (though it is more than that) as imputed righteousness.

Justification as Imputed Righteousness

To impute means to ascribe vicariously. In this instance, imputed righteousness is the righteousness of Jesus Christ attributed to us by virtue of our faith in him. It is not our own righteousness; it is his righteousness attributed to our account so that God sees us through the righteousness of an only Son.

That would be like . . . murdering an only child, and the parents saying, "We not only forgive you for murdering our only child, we want you to have that child's inheritance."

Imagine, Jesus of Nazareth was so sensitized to whom God is that prevenient grace did its work to perfection enabling him to overcome the law of sin and death so that Satan had no right to take his life. Only Satan's arrogance could have led to such a mistake, a mistake as big as the lie told to Adam and Eve. This mistake would lead to the cure for all our mistakes so that our acceptance of Jesus Christ as sacrifice for sin is eternal in the heavens.

Now, our sins are pardoned, forgiven, covered over and rooted out. It is as if God were saying, "You crucified my only Son because if you were the only one to have sinned since the beginning of time, Jesus would still have gone to the cross. I not only forgive you for crucifying my Son, however, I want you to have His inheritance." That would be like breaking into someone's home, murdering an only child, and the parents saying, "We not only forgive you for murdering our only child, we want you to have that child's inheritance." You would probably think one of two things of those parents — either they were raving mad or they were for real. Somehow God's love is for real and that kind of love can be trusted.

Just before last Christmas I saw a cartoon featuring a small child saying, "Let's see if I've got this straight. It is Jesus' birthday, but I get the presents, right?" In the next caption the child smiles, saying, "Is this a great religion or what!" It is indeed a great religion, but most of us have a way to go before living up to it.

Justification as a Relative Change

Relative implies comparative, not absolute. With regard to justification, the term "relative" reminds us that we are not yet perfect. In fact, we are probably as far away from "obedience" as we will ever be. Justification simply marks the point at which we reverse the plunge toward disobedience. Just as the process prior to conversion is not three steps backward and no steps forward (it is more like three steps backward for every two steps forward), the process after conversion is not three steps forward and no steps backward (it is more like three steps forward for every two steps backward).

Too much of the time some Christians would seem to suggest that to be Christian is to achieve perfection. That is the kiss of death. Christians are not necessarily perfect, just forgiven.

> *Too much of the time some Christians would seem to suggest that to be Christian is to achieve perfection. That is the kiss of death.*

I once served a church with more than 6,000 members. Some people suggested that we had a church full of hypocrites. I simply responded, "Yes, but if you think they are hypocrites now, you should have seen them before we got 'em." Christianity does not make hypocrites non-hypocrites; it makes them less hypocritical. For that matter, and even more significantly, Christianity does not make Christians better than non-Christians, it makes them better than what they were. In fact, I have some Christian friends that are far more difficult to get along with than some of my non-Christian friends. But, you think my Christian friends are difficult to get along with now, you should have seen them before. They were something to behold. *Hah! Explains a lot.*

Justification may be relative, but the Spirit is at work and God sees our potential, not just our present condition. How else could Jesus brag on a bunch of Bedouin disciples in John 17: "They are not of the world any more than I am of the world." Even as he spoke they were sleeping when they should have been praying. En route to the place of prayer they argued as to who would be first in the Kingdom of God. Within the hour they would desert him to the man. Jesus was not bragging on their present station but on the direction in which they were headed — Pentecost. That is the story that must be told following our concluding section on justification.

→ God writes w/ a different perspective

Justification as Entitling Us To Heaven

Without the righteousness of Christ we can have no claim to glory; without holiness we could have no fitness for it.

John Wesley writes,

> The righteousness of Christ is doubtless necessary for any soul that enters into glory: But so is personal holiness too, for every child of man. But it is highly needful to be observed, that they are necessary in different respects. The former is necessary to *entitle* us to heaven; the latter to *qualify* us for it. Without the righteousness of Christ we can have no *claim* to glory; without holiness we could have no *fitness* for it. By the former we become members of Christ, children of God, and heirs of the kingdom of heaven. By the latter "we are made meet to be partakers of the inheritance of the saints in light."[6]

HEB.10 we are made perfect forever even as we are being made holy

This quotation anticipates our next chapters, but before we enter those discussions we must state once again what Wesley means by justification. The righteousness of Jesus Christ puts us right with God so that we are entitled to a right relationship with a loving God. Not that we *earn* such a relationship, we certainly do not. Someone has said that mercy means that we do not receive what we do deserve (God's punishment); whereas grace means that we do receive what we do not deserve (God's salvation). Though we are not yet "qualified" to enjoy heaven (that comes with sanctification), we are "entitled" to enter heaven by faith in the blood of Jesus.

Review

If conversion could be understood as an exchange of the "law of sin and death" for the "Law of the Spirit of life" (Romans 8:2), justification sets us free from the Law devoid of the Spirit and without the power nor the inclination to obey it. It sets us free from the bondage of the Law which is impossible to obey out of our own resources. Justification turns us from a view of the universe where we are at its center and prepares us for a view of the universe where God is at its center. Justification, therefore, prepares us for the new birth, for Wesley the other side of conversion.

Study Questions:

1. What are the characteristics of justification?
2. What is the significance of sacrifice in the Old Testament? What problem does it present in regard to overcoming sin?
3. How does the sacrifice of Jesus Christ resolve that problem?
4. What is imputed righteousness?
5. How is justification a "relative" change?

Notes

[1] Wesley's *Works*, Vol. 5, pp. 223f.

[2] An interesting article on "expiate" in Kittle, *Theological Dictionary of the New Testament* (Vol. 3, p. 317), argues convincingly that what "*man*" offers in the Old Testament *propitiates*; what "*God*" offers in the New Testament *expiates*.

³Wesley's *Works*, Vol. 5, p. 55.

⁴Wesley's *Works*, Vol. 7, p. 313.

⁵Wesley's *Works*, Vol. 5, p. 57.

⁶Wesley's *Works*, Vol. 7, p. 314.

Leviticus 4:13-21;   *Acts 1:5*
19:18   *Romans 5:5; 8:16*
John 3:3; 15:1-5

The new birth is the side of conversion that denotes a turning to *righteousness — what God does* in *us by the Holy Spirit. It is the* beginning of *an imparted righteousness or that which is realized in us through the power of the Holy Spirit — a real change. In most instances Wesley would have associated the outset of this transformation into the likeness of Jesus Christ (2 Corinthians 3:18) with the "baptism of the Holy Spirit."*

1. The new birth turns us *to* righteousness.
2. The believer is clensed of sin or washed by the blood of Jesus Christ.
3. The indwelling power of the Holy Spirit then gives the believer victory over sin begins the process of recovering our "original righteousness."

CHAPTER

8

Where grace as the work of the Holy Spirit is concerned, this chapter is truly pivotal. In fact, some might pick up the book for this chapter alone. The terms "new

The New Birth: Baptism in the Holy Spirit

birth" and (as I have identified it here), "baptism in the Holy Spirit" attract that kind of attention. Be that as it may and as important as the new birth/baptism in the Holy Spirit is, this is not the final chapter. Please keep that in mind. Without all that is to follow the new birth/Holy Spirit baptism could serve only to condemn. "To those whom much has been given; much is required." So read this chapter carefully but keep on reading. "A tree is recognized by its fruit" (Matthew 12:33).

The new birth has already been identified as the second phase of conversion. Just as justification is the turning *from* sin (the *terminus-a-quo*), the new birth/Holy Spirit baptism is turning *to* righteousness (the *terminus-ad-quem*). Just as justification is objective/forensic or legal, the new birth/Holy Spirit baptism is subjective/personal. If justification is God *for* us, then the new birth/Holy Spirit baptism is God *in* us. Since justification is imputed righteousness, a relative change, entitling us to heaven, the new birth/Holy Spirit baptism is the *beginning* of imparted righteousness, a real change, qualifying us for heaven. After I have attempted to establish a case for the identification of the new birth with the baptism in the Holy Spirit, I will respond to each of these characteristics separately.

The New Birth as Baptism in the Holy Spirit

Without belaboring mere terms, the phrase "the baptism of the Holy Ghost" (as far as I can tell) was first coined by John Fletcher and is, in fact, indexed in his *Works*. Fletcher has already been described, just in passing, as John Wesley's appointed successor had Wesley not outlived him.

> *As far as I can tell, the phrase "the baptism of the Holy Ghost" was first coined by John Fletcher.*

John Fletcher (1729-1785) was born to a highly respected family in Nyon, Switzerland, educated in Geneva and immigrated to England in 1752 where, as an Anglican priest, he soon became a Methodist. Called by some the "Methodist Mystic" or the "Shropshire Saint," Fletcher's contribution to the formation of Methodist theology was considerable. Of particular interest here is that he not only systematized the works of John Wesley, he also provided his own unique understanding of Christian Perfection by incorporating a doctrine of the baptism of the Holy Ghost (from this point on referred to as Holy Spirit baptism).

Fletcher's interest in Holy Spirit baptism arose primarily from his defense of Wesley's doctrine of Christian perfection against a form of Calvinism which tended to lean toward antinomianism (defined in our Introduction as the blatant disregard for the Law). Educated in Geneva, Fletcher was well acquainted with Calvin's (to use a Wesleyan phrase) "overgrown fear of Popery." Fletcher believed with Wesley that the Reformers (Wesley referred to both Luther and Calvin as "silly saints") exalted the doctrine of justification by faith to the discouragement, if not the exclusion, of good works. Although

Methodists clearly insist on salvation by faith alone, faith has its inevitable fruit. Wesley himself writes in a letter to Elizabeth Bennis that one of the Methodists

> preaches salvation by faith in the same manner that my brother and I have done; and as Mr. Fletcher (one of the finest writers of the age) has beautifully explained it. None of us talk of being accepted for our works: That is the Calvinist slander. But we all maintain, we are not saved without works; that works are a conditon (though not the meritorious cause) of final salvation. It is by faith in the righteousness and blood of Christ that we are enabled to do all good works; and it is for the sake of these that all who fear God and work righteousness are accepted of Him.[1]

Fletcher had added his pen to that of Wesley's during the predestination/free will controversies of the late 1760s and early 1770s. In publishing his *Checks to Antinomianism* he notes,

> ... it appears if I am not mistaken that we stand now as much in need of a reformation from antinomianism as our ancestors did of a reformation from popery. People, it seems, may now be "in Christ" without being "new creatures" without casting "old things" away. They may be God's children without God's image; and "born of the Spirit" without the "fruits of the Spirit."[2]

In light of this last statement (although necessarily anticipating the chapters to follow) we should make at least some brief reference to Fletcher's application of the work of the Holy Spirit to Wesley's doctrine of Christian perfection. The first three *Checks* basically defend Wesley's doctrine of perfection. The *Fourth Check*, however, uses the language of Pentecost to describe a process of Holy Spirit baptism/perfection as a number of experiences culminating in entire sanctification.[3]

In a sermon outline for the text Acts 1:5: "For John baptized with water, but in a few days you will be baptized with the Holy Spirit," Fletcher discusses the general necessity of Holy Spirit baptism. Basically we are helpless and unfit for heaven or bliss without God's Holy Spirit to empower us. Water baptism alone serves only to condemn without "a fresh baptism, till the Holy Ghost, *which is grace*, fill your soul."[4]

Interestingly, John Wesley (as we shall soon see) described the new birth in terms nearly identical to Fletcher's Holy Spirit baptism. Obviously one had influence upon the other. Although Wesley believed that Holy Spirit baptism normally occurs at the moment of regeneration or new birth and insisted that any *subsequent* baptisms of Fletcher's were "not scriptural and not quite proper; for they all received the Holy Ghost when they were justified," he greatly appreciated Fletcher's overall thrust.[5] For both (although again we are anticipating chapters to follow) perfection was clearly a *process* following the new birth.

Fletcher sees Holy Spirit baptism repeated in a succession of experiences beginning with the new birth and concluding in glory.

For Wesley, this "going on to perfection" following the new birth was linked with the all important doctrine of perseverance, and Holy Spirit baptism initiated and sustained the process of perfection as a continuing experience of that new birth. For Fletcher, Holy Spirit baptism initiated and sustained the process of perfection as a number of experiences within and subsequent to the new birth. In short, Fletcher sees Holy Spirit baptism repeated in a succession of experiences beginning with the new birth and concluding in glory. Appropriately, he writes,

> Should you ask, How many baptisms or effusions of the sanctifying Spirit are necessary to cleanse a believer from all sin, and to kindle his soul into perfect love? I reply, that the effect of a sanctifying truth depending upon the ardour of the faith in which the truth is embraced, and upon the power of the Spirit with which it is applied, I should betray a want of modesty if I brought the operations of the Holy Ghost, and the energy of faith, under a rule which is not expressly laid down in the Scriptures . . . .
> If one powerful baptism of the Spirit "seal you unto the

day of redemption," and cleanse you from all "moral filthiness," so much the better. If two, or more, be necesssary, the Lord can repeat them; "his arm is not shortened that it cannot save;" nor is his promise of the Spirit stinted.[6]

Although Wesley would obviously agree with the overall sentiments here, terms sometimes get in the way. In a letter written to his "wife to be," Mary Bosanquet, on March 7, 1778, Fletcher expresses his differences with Wesley in these words:

You will find my views of this matter in Mr. Wesley's sermons on Christian Perfection and on Spiritual Christianity; with this difference, that I would distinguish more exactly between the believers baptized with the Pentecostal power of the Holy Ghost, and the believers who, like the Apostles after our Lord's ascension, are not yet filled with that power.[7]

It occurs to me that the point of all this is (or should be) clear. John Fletcher coined the phrase "Holy Spirit baptism" (actually "the baptism of the Holy Ghost") to describe the power of the Holy Spirit available through any number of experiences to every believer for going on to perfection subsequent to the new birth. Similarly, John Wesley, although not using the term Holy Spirit baptism as such, described the new birth as the power of the Holy Spirit available in a single experience to every believer for going on to perfection concomitant within (or accompanying) the new birth.

> *Both Wesley and Fletcher believed in an experience of being filled with the Holy Spirit.*

Both Wesley and Fletcher believed in an experience of being filled with the Holy Spirit. Fletcher used the phrase Holy Spirit baptism, and Wesley used the phrase new birth. All of the characteristics in the sections to follow are common to both experiences. Although Wesley and Fletcher disagree as to the number of experiences and perhaps as to the moment of empowerment, both strongly affirm the necessity of the Holy Spirit's power (the grace of God) for "walking out the land" as an "altogether Christian." Let's look closer.

New Birth / Holy Spirit Baptism as the Turning to Righteousness

Anyone with even a beginner's understanding of John Wesley knows that he was dead serious about holiness. Wesley also believed that the Reformers' doctrine of justification undermined their doctrine of sanctification. For that reason Wesley was determined to get beyond Martin Luther's *"simul justus, simul peccator"* ("the same time justified, the same time a sinner"). In fact, Wesley was so sensitive to this issue that he was nearly obsessed with the notion that Methodists would not make a mockery of this or any other Evangelical doctrine. He strongly believed that the doctrines of justification and salvation by faith had been grievously abused by many of the people called Methodist. He would not have it! He writes,

> Frankly, there are times when I find more profit in sermons on either good tempers or good works than in what are vulgarly called Gospel sermons. That term is now become a mere cant word. I wish none in our Society would use it. It has no determinate meaning. Let but a pert, self-sufficient animal, that has neither sense nor grace, bawl out something about Christ and his blood or justification by faith, and his hearers cry out, "What a fine Gospel sermon!" — surely the Methodists have not so learnt Christ. *We know no Gospel without salvation from sin.*"[8]

Furthermore, after turning *from* sin, we must then turn *to* (the term *terminus-ad-quem* implies a turning *to*) righteousness. It was terribly important to Wesley that justification manifest itself in a new birth that was the *beginning* of sanctification. Obviously the operative word here is not only sanctification but "beginning." The corner had been turned, but the Christian had not yet arrived — not by a longshot!

True, the Holy Spirit has now moved within the believer with power and effect, but sin, though it no longer reigns, still remains. New birth is the story of humankind coming to God the *Abba* (or Parent) through God the Son, and the vortex where these two come together creates the incredible energy of the Holy Spirit. Now, however, the power of that Spirit must seek the mind of Christ. Grace abounds as the noun (that is all the other verbs as well), but faith must now "walk the talk." Like the story of Balaam in Numbers 22, the Spirit has not only opened the donkey's mouth but also the prophet's eyes so that the vision of personal and social holiness is clearly before us.

New Birth / Holy Spirit Baptism as Subjective / Personal

Pentecost was a highly personal experience. As a result of the objective work of Jesus Christ on the cross, the atonement had been "paid in full" (literally "it is finished," the exact words of Jesus on the cross). The banquet invitations could now be announced. Those who would believe that Jesus is the Christ, the son of the living God, would be *baptized by the Holy Spirit into the body of Jesus Christ* and *empowered to obey his commands*. In effect, there were no Christians prior to Pentecost. Oh, there were people in right relationship with God, but there were no Christians, as such, since to be a Christian is not only to be a descendant of Abraham; but, once again, to be baptized by the Holy Spirit into the body of Jesus Christ, *his Church*, and empowered to bear fruit.

> *There were no Christians prior to Pentecost.*

Within the context of his "Farewell Discourse," Jesus clearly outlines the work of the Holy Spirit,

> I am the true vine, and my Father is the gardener. He cuts off every branch in me that bears no fruit, while every branch that does bear fruit he prunes so that it will be even more fruitful . . . . No branch can bear fruit by itself; it must remain in the vine. Neither can you bear fruit unless you remain in me . . . ; apart from me you can do nothing.[9]

Jesus goes on to say in that same passage that to bear fruit is first of all to obey his commands by loving each other as he has loved us. Seem impossible? Remember, that with God all things are possible.

In light of that fact, the two Scripture passages that are perhaps most crucial to the work of the Holy Spirit as a result of the Holy Spirit's baptism are Romans 8:16: "The Spirit himself testifies with our spirit that we are God's children" (John Wesley's favorite text), and Romans 5:5: "And hope does not disappoint us, because God has poured out his love into our hearts by the Holy Spirit, whom he has given us." Let's be more specific.

New Birth / Holy Spirit Baptism
as the Beginning of Imparted Righteousness

Imparted righteousness is the righteousness of Jesus Christ, not simply attributed to us (as in imputed righteousness), but realized in us. Although one of the operative words here is still "beginning," when the Holy Spirit comes into our lives to dwell, just as grace begets grace, faith begets faith so that we know that we are the children of God (Romans 8:16).

Slowly but surely (albeit, perhaps more slowly than surely) we gain more and more confidence as to who and what we are becoming. The Holy Spirit (or the Spirit that makes us holy) increasingly grants us the mind of Christ so that (like Christ), "we know that we know that we know." Too frequently I am reminded by those around me that when our sense of the reality of God grows dim we tend to fall apart within and fall against each other without, only to swing blindly back and forth between boredom and violence. Little wonder many of us define "spirituality" as an awareness of God's presence in my life. I am spiritual almost to the precise degree that I am aware of God's presence in my life. It is tough to sin (or to sit and do nothing) with God looking at you.

Similarly, when the Holy Spirit comes into our lives to dwell, we begin to see people as God sees them (Romans 5:5). We begin to see people as one would see one's own children.

A few years ago during a service of worship I was given only 30 seconds notice on what I sometimes refer to as "the dreaded children's sermon." It is not that I do not believe that such sermons are important; I do, but without adequate time to prepare I tend to panic. It is difficult to think like a five-year-old even though I have had several in my own home. As the children were coming forward I remember praying, "God this is an emergency; I need help *now*; five minutes from now is too late." Within seconds, 50 or 60 children were gathered around, daring me to bore them. I did something that I had never done before and will probably never do again. I asked them if they had pets. Most did.

In fact, a child named Brian, sitting right next to me, looked up and said, "I have two cats." Then much to my surprise he added, "No, strike that, I have one cat; the garage door got the other one."

Not quite knowing how to respond, I simply said how sorry I was that the garage door had killed one of his cats, only to hear him say, "Oh, that's OK. That cat is in heaven, and I still have the other one."

Within seconds, 50 or 60 children were gathered around, daring me to bore them.

Then it occurred to me to ask a question, "Brian, who loves your remaining cat more, you or me?"

He answered without a blink, "That's a stupid question, I love that cat more." When I asked why, he simply retorted, "I spend more time with that cat."

Then it occurred to me to ask another question, "Brian, who loves *you* more, your mother and father or me?"

Brian thought that was another stupid question and quickly replied, "My mom and dad."

Again when I asked why, he responded as before, "Because I spend more time with them."

I then just as quickly replied, "And because you are a part of them. It is the most natural thing in the world to love that which is a part of you." Then turning to all of the children's parents in the congregation I reminded them that they loved these children like I could never love them. Why? Wonderfully, the children responded in one voice, "Because we are a part of them."

I simply added, "True, and if you don't believe that just try and find a parking space in the grammar school parking lot on the evening of the Christmas pageant."

Then returning to Brian I asked him to give me the largest number that he could imagine. After some thought, he said, "Thirty trillion" (which is not bad when you consider that that is 10 times the national debt).

"Brian," I then said, "take your mother and father's love for you and multiply it by 30 trillion. (It should have been infinity, but this was all that he could handle.) That's how much God loves you because you are far more a part of God than you are a part of your mom and dad." I then dismissed them asking them to think about this, rejoicing that God had somehow been a part of that whole experience.

Nevertheless, imagine my surprise when following my "adult" sermon the Spirit of God gave me this invitation for concluding the service: "Would all of you good people please put your faith and trust in Jesus Christ so we can all go to heaven and be with Brian's other cat." Well, you might chuckle, but I was at the communion rail for nearly an hour praying with those who were coming forward. Even Brian went to his parents and asked just how much it would cost to fly to Chicago; he wanted to come and visit me. We are still close friends. So, what's the point? God loves us and the Holy Spirit enables us to love as God loves. That is what the beginning of imparted righteousness is all about.

> *"Would all of you good people please put your faith and trust in Jesus Christ so we can all go to heaven and be with Brian's other cat."*

The Beginning of a Real Change, Qualifying Us for Heaven

Remember, if justification is a relative change entitling us to heaven, then the new birth/Holy Spirit baptism is the beginning of a real change qualifying us for heaven. The Law (once the Law of sin and death) now empowered by the Spirit becomes the Law of the Spirit of life, so that we have both the power and the inclination to obey it. We are at once alive to the Law that previously served only to bring condemnation and death. Furthermore, to be alive is the one great desire of countless people. Life without passion is simply one moment following another soon to be forgotten.

Recently a man on the brink of middle age confessed to me that as an international journalist he had lived in all of the exotic places and experienced all of the "thrills" so that he could no longer feel passion about anything. Imagine being 35 and nowhere to go but down. His urgent request for prayer was that God would somehow renew his sense of excitement about the "meaningful life." Who can blame him? He needs the Holy Spirit's baptism available in the new birth, and I told him so. He's considering. Consider if you must, but eventually not to decide is to decide. One can only be a "seeker" for so long before agnosticism turns into atheism. Let God arise indeed.

> *Imagine being 35 and nowhere to go but down.*

The new birth/Holy Spirit baptism completes the conversion experience but marks only the beginning of one's walk with God. The forgiveness of sins past has now embraced the power to overcome sins future. Objective righteousness begins to embrace a subjective righteousness, *both personal and social, individual and systemic.* The emphasis here supplies the key for the entire third part of our study of law and grace within the context of a Wesleyan theology of grace.

Overcoming sin, abolishing strongholds, is a never-ending adventure. Although Wesley talked about "entire sanctification," he was never complacent or even content. One could never afford to stop growing. In fact, he taught that those "perfected" grew even more rapidly than those not yet so blessed. Holiness was Wesley's constant passion. Holiness, however, was always linked with overcoming sin in persons *and* systems.

I am sometimes accused of speaking too much about social justice or speaking out too strongly about some justice issue. You cannot speak too much about social justice. That is precisely what the baptism of the Holy Spirit is all about. I've paid my dues with regard to the grace available only through faith in Jesus Christ. Now let's do something with it. The first book I wrote many years ago had a chapter entitled, "Battleships in Mudpuddles." I still like that image.

Many of us assume that Wesley made frequent reference to Leviticus because of its emphasis on holiness (the word "holy" appears more times in Leviticus than in any other biblical book). We forget that "Love your neighbor as yourself" (Leviticus 19:18) introduces a whole host of social concerns affecting both the individual and the community. In fact there is a sin offering for both individual and community (cf. Lev. 4:13-21). In other words, the individual not only sins, but the community or nation also sins and must repent and make sacrifice. The baptism of the Holy Spirit links love with obedience, faith with work, salvation with judgment.

> *"Love your neighbor as yourself" introduces a whole host of social concerns affecting both the individual and the community.*

Again, while the world is still mildly interested, we have got to make certain that we are "walking the talk," that the baptism of the Holy Spirit is empowering a vision that is worthy of Christ himself. Those well worn words from the pen of John Wesley still haunt me on occasion: "I am not afraid that the people called Methodists should ever cease to exist either in Europe or America. But I am afraid, lest they should only exist as a dead sect, having the form of religion without the power."[10] Nor do we want the power without the form. Oh, for balance! God give us both. May their tribe increase together!

Review

Many have understood Wesley's views on the baptism in the Holy Spirit differently. Some associate Wesley's doctrine of entire sanctification (not the new birth) with Holy Spirit baptism. I believe that this cannot be supported in light of Wesley's own description of the new birth and in light of John Fletcher's description of the Holy Spirit's baptism. Again, they are so similar it suggests that one had influence upon the other. Even more important, with conversion the corner is turned. The believer is now being restored to an original righteousness that has implications for both persons and systems. The Spirit moves within the believer and the church with power and effect. The Law of sin and death is now the Law of the Spirit of life. At long last, grace is in control and obedience is our goal.

Study Questions:

1. Can you contrast justification and the new birth?
2. Can you describe the new birth in relation to the baptism of the Holy Spirit?
3. What is the significance of the word "beginning" in the definition of the new birth?
4. What is the connection between Romans 5:5, Romans 8:16 and the work of the Spirit?
5. What is the significance of the work of the Holy Spirit in individuals and systems for social as well as personal holiness?

Notes

[1]Wesley's *Works*, Vol. 12, p. 399.

[2]Cited in John A. Knight, "John Fletcher's Influence on the Development of Wesleyan Theology in America," *Wesleyan Theological Journal* (Spring, 1978), XIV, p. 15.

[3]Fletcher, *Works*, Vol. 1, p. 160. Cited in Timothy L. Smith, "How John Fletcher Became the Theologian of Wesleyan Perfectionism 1770–1776," *Wesleyan Theological Journal* (Spring 1980), XIV, p. 73. Professor Smith here interprets (or perhaps misinterprets) one brief statement from Fletcher to imply that Holy Spirit baptism can be equated with entire sanctification. Cf. Wesley's response in *Works*, Vol. 12, p. 416.

[4]Fletcher, *Works*, Vol. 8, pp. 464f. Italics mine.

[5]Wesley's *Works*, Vol. 12, p. 416. Cf. David L. Cubie, "Perfection in Wesley and Fletcher: Inaugural or Teleological?" *Wesleyan Theological Journal* (Spring, 1976), XII, p. 24.

[6]Fletcher, *Checks to Antinominanism* (New York: Carlton and Proter, n.d.), Vol. 11, p. 632.

[7]Cited in Luke Tyerman, *Wesley's Designated Successor* (New York: A. C. Armstrong & Son, 1886), p. 411.

[8]Wesley, *Letters* (Telford, ed.), Vol. 6, pp. 326f.

[9]John 15:1-5.

[10]Wesley's *Works*, Vol. 13, p. 258.

PART III:
THE LAW OF THE SPIRIT OF LIFE

The Law of the Spirit of Life is the law (the same law as before) now enlivened by the Spirit so that Christians have both the power and the inclination to obey it — the result is obedience. Sanctifying grace prevails.

OBEDIENCE

Physical Death   Original Righteousness/
Physical Birth

Entire Sanctification   Infant Baptism

CARNAL
NATURE   Actual Sin

Fruit
Gifts

THE LAW OF
THE SPIRIT
OF LIFE
(love)

SANCTIFYING
GRACE
PREVAILS

ORIGINAL SIN
PREVAILS

THE LAW OF SIN
AND DEATH
(fear)

PREVENIENT
GRACE

New Birth   Justification

Justifying Grace

DISOBEDIENCE

Matthew 16:18-19, 25
Luke 15:11-32; 20:1-16

Romans, chapters 6-8
2 Corinthians 10:3-4
Galatians 5:22-23
Hebrews 12:2

Sanctifying grace denotes the work of the Holy Spirit in the believer between conversion and death. Accompanied by fruit and gifts, sanctifying grace slowly but surely roots out those things that would separate Christians from God, themselves, and those around them.

1. Sanctifying grace is the power of the Holy Spirit setting us aside and then empowering us for ministry in God's Kingdom.

2. The law of the Spirit of life sets us free from the law of sin and death.

3. Sanctifying grace creates a new vision for individual and church for overcoming sin in persons and systems.

CHAPTER

9

As a result of the power of the Holy Spirit available through faith in Jesus Christ, the law of sin and death has now become the law of the Spirit of life. Remember, the

Sanctifying Grace: Overcoming Sin in Persons and Systems

gospel is good news/bad news/good news. Original righteousness succumbs to original sin (and subsequently actual sin) which yields to justifying and sanctifying grace. Sanctifying grace (as we shall see in

Chapter 12) then ultimately fulfills the law. Although the tide has turned, the final good news has only just begun, however. The Holy Spirit now dwells within but must continue to operate as sanctifying grace until the work is complete.

The blood of Jesus Christ has broken the power of sin and restored the Christian to fellowship with God. The work of the Holy Spirit can now prevail, returning us to our original righteousness, our created image — the goal of sanctifying grace.

After defining and clarifying a few terms, we will then address this important doctrine under these headings:

The Law of the Spirit of Life, New Beginnings, and Overcoming Sin in Persons and Systems.

Sanctifying Grace Defined

To sanctify is to cleanse or purify and then to set aside for special use. Grace, you recall, denotes the work of the Holy Spirit. Sanctifying grace, therefore, is the Holy Spirit (or the Spirit that makes us holy) cleansing and setting apart for ministry in the "kingdom of God." Sanctifying grace is the Holy Spirit at work in individuals and in communities of believers taking back the land now ruled by the Enemy — the evil one. Again, 1 John 5:19 states clearly (if not tragically) that "the whole world is under the control of the evil one." Without God's help we are without hope in the world. By grace through faith, however, everyone born of God loves and obeys God's commands and *overcomes* the world and its present ruler.

Sanctifying grace moves the individual away from disobedience and back toward obedience. Sanctifying grace moves the universal body of Christ, the Church, away from things that diminish, discourage and destroy and back toward establishing God's eternal rule "on earth as it is in heaven." Sanctifying grace moves away from law as sin and death and towards law as the Spirit of life.

The Law of the Spirit of Life

As Christians, what do we believe about how God relates to creation? Did God act one way in the Old Testament and another in the New? Is Old Testament law bad and New Testament grace good? From a Judeo/Christian point of view, how does the law as interpreted by the Mishna and the Talmud (the Jewish commentary on the Law) differ from the same law as interpreted by the New Testament? If Christians interpret the law through the life and teachings of Jesus (he is our Mishna and our Talmud), what difference does it make?

> *God challenges us, "If you can describe your vision, I can predict your future; for the people without a vision perish."*

Once again Romans 8:1-2 provides the key: "Therefore, there is now no condemnation for those who are in Christ Jesus, because through Christ Jesus the law of the Spirit of life set me free from the law of sin and death." The same Old Testament law that was sin and death prior to conversion is now, in Christ, enlivened by the Spirit so that we have both the power and inclination to obey it. It becomes the law of the Spirit of life.

The law of the Spirit of life means that God is with us. Even in this moment God is preparing the way.

New Testament grace insists that the Old Testament law creates a vision within persons and the Church for establishing God's eternal rule throughout the world. God has more invested in our ministry than we do. God challenges us, "If you can describe your vision, I can predict your future; for the people without a vision perish." Do not be discouraged. The law of the Spirit of life means that God is with us. Even in this moment God is preparing the way.

One of the greatest sins for the nation Israel was its refusal to take the land. The children of Israel allowed themselves to be discouraged and were sentenced to 38 more years wandering in the wilderness. In hopes of encouraging you (increasing your vision, not your burden), let me tell you a part of that saga along with "the rest of the story."

Eighteen months after leaving Egypt the children of Israel, gathered around the mountain in the Sinai, had received the Law (twice) and had organized more than two million people into 12 ruling tribes. They had built the Tabernacle to exact specifications and had received their marching orders to "take the land" promised to their ancestors. Although it was normally an 11-day journey, it took them two months to reach the southern border of a land flowing with milk and honey. Twelve spies were immediately sent out to devise the best route for taking the land which God had prepared and promised.

After 40 days, 10 of these spies returned with a bad report. They complained that there were giants in the land and by comparison they were like grasshoppers. Within hours the entire nation had become discouraged despite the minority report of Joshua and Caleb stating that the land could be taken if they would but obey God and proceed. So, the moment to advance passed. Though some repented of their lack of faith, it was too late. The entire nation was sentenced to 38 more years wandering in the wilderness.

During those years a generation perished in the desert. Now, however, the children of Israel were encamped on the plains of Moab, once again poised to take the land, wondering whether or not God was still with them, if the covenant was still valid.

> *Then the real miracle takes place. The Lord opened the eyes of the internationally-known pagan prophet so that he, too, now sees the angel . . .*

Balak, the king of Moab, was more than a little concerned about so many Israelites encamped within his borders and decided (there being too many to fight) to summon an internationally-known pagan prophet named Balaam to come and curse these intruders. Since Balaam did not want to make the long journey, Balak had to make several overtures before Balaam could be persuaded to get on his donkey and set out for Moab.

En route, an angel of the Lord with a drawn sword stands in the narrow gorge through which Balaam must pass. Although Balaam does not see the angel, his donkey does and realizing that his master is in danger, balks. Balaam, not understanding, goads the animal only to have the donkey balk again and finally sit down as Balaam beats the beast unmercifully.

At this point the Lord God opens the donkey's mouth. The donkey does not say anything terribly profound (we give that donkey far too much credit), but he does say words to the effect, "Listen, Balaam, don't you realize that I am out of character here? Have I ever balked or sat down on you before?" After Balaam admits that the donkey had never done such before, the donkey adds, "Open your eyes. There is an angel of the Lord standing there with a drawn sword about to strike."

Then the real miracle takes place. The Lord opened the eyes of the internationally-known pagan prophet so that he, too, now sees the angel who warns, "You may continue on your journey, but you must speak only what I tell you to speak." Balaam then joins Balak, but when he opens his mouth to curse the Israelites he can speak only blessings, *seven* of them. Although the last three are a tad thin, the first four are literally packed with words of encouragement from on high. For example, this is one of the first times in the Bible that God is referred to as the nation's sovereign:

Look! I have received a command to bless them,
For God has blessed them,
And I cannot reverse it!
He has not seen sin in Jacob.
He will not trouble Israel!
Jehovah their God is with them.
He is their king!

Numbers 23:20-21 (*The Living Bible*).

Similarly, Balaam's oracles contain one of the earliest references to the Messiah. Again:

I see in the future of Israel,
Far down the distant trail,
That there shall come a star from Jacob!
This ruler of Israel
Shall smite the people of Moab,
And destroy the sons of Sheth.
Israel shall possess all Edom and Seir.
They shall overcome their enemies.

Numbers 24:17-18a (*The Living Bible*).

In effect, God is using the mouth of an internationally-known pagan prophet (so well-known that oracles from Balaam can be found outside of the Scriptures) to remind the children of Israel that God is still with them.

Many of us today may feel as if we, too, are camped on the plains of Moab, looking across the Jordan, wondering whether God is still with us. I assure you, God is still with us. I do not wish to play the role of pagan prophet (much less of talking donkey), but I can tell you with confidence that all of us stand on the brink of a new beginning as we repent and renew our faith in Jesus Christ. Let me illustrate.

New Beginnings

We have already stated that true spirituality is more repent and believe than grunt and groan. Let me now expand on a concept mentioned toward the end of Part I. Remember the principle of high pressure, low pressure? In the silence deep within you, allow the Holy Spirit to plumb some new depth of your experience, to reveal some area of resistance, some aspect of life not yet yielded to God. Then as you repent and believe, allow God to move to that low pressure and take that sin from you. Our willingness for God to take sin from us, not our ability to give it to God, is the key. If we were able to give it to God, we would not need God. Will power alone would be sufficient.

> *Our willingness for God to take sin from us, not our ability to give it to God, is the key.*

Although will power alone is not sufficient, do not despair. Grace, the indwelling power of the Holy Spirit, changes our attitude toward God and sin so that we are now righteousness prone. Our inclination is to obey rather than to disobey God. The next time we are tempted after "repent and believe," it is actually easier to obey than to disobey God. Christianity is just that practical. Patterns of disobedience created by years of yielding to sin can now be broken.

Always Conqueror

John Wesley writes after his evangelical conversion,

> I was much buffeted with temptations; but cried out, and they fled away. They returned again and again. I as often lifted up my eyes, and He 'sent me help from his holy place.' And herein I found the difference between this and my former state chiefly consisted. I was striving, yea, fighting with, all my might under the law, as well as under grace. But then I was sometimes, if not often, conquered; now, I was always conqueror.[1]

Along those same lines the apostle Paul writes in Romans 7 (remember that *all* of Romans 6-8 is speaking of sanctifying grace) that the sinful or carnal nature still hangs around even after conversion. Although sin no longer reigns; it still remains. The law continues to do its work by making sin "utterly sinful," reminding me that nothing good lives "*in my sinful nature*" (vv. 13-18).

Paul confesses that even as a Christian, though

> I have the desire to do what is good; I cannot (on my own) carry it out. For what I do is not the good I want to do; no, the evil I do not want to do — this I keep on doing . . . Who will rescue me from this body of death? Thanks be to God — through Jesus Christ our Lord! (Romans 7:18-19, 24-25)[2]

It should not surprise us that Paul moves immediately into the passage quoted earlier where the law of sin and death is overcome by the law of the Spirit of life for those who are "in Christ Jesus." Grace must not only save; grace must also sustain. No condemnation, indeed.

I frequently find myself praying a prayer behind a prayer: "Lord God, I want to want what you want for me!" Truly, we are "treasure in jars of clay to show that this all-surpassing power is from God and not from us. We are hard pressed on every side, but not crushed; perplexed, but not in despair; persecuted, but not abandoned; struck down, but not destroyed" (2 Corinthians 4:7-9). In other words, our insufficiency reveals (or perhaps proves) God's all sufficiency.

Dante said, "Sin is any good thing loved inordinately."

One of the most basic principles of law and grace is that one does not overcome sin by trying to overcome sin. The law in and of itself is religion on the *defense*. Like my alcoholic friend introduced at the end of Part I, law compounds sin and consumes us; we succumb to the law of sin and death. Again, Paul confesses that "sin, seizing the opportunity afforded by the commandment, produced in me every kind of covetous desire" (Romans 7:8). Under the law even good becomes distorted. Dante said, "Sin is any good thing loved inordinately." Grace, on the other hand, is religion on the *offense*. It gets our eyes off the sin and fixes our eyes on Jesus, "the author and perfecter of our faith" (Hebrews 12:2). If sin is compounded under law, it loses its appeal under grace. The best way to stop thinking about sin is to start thinking about Jesus. Grace redirects our attention.

Grace implies fresh starts, new beginnings. No matter what we have done, there is no condemnation for those who are in Christ Jesus. *Not that sin does not have its consequences.* That has already been established. We have only to remember Moses, or Sampson, or David, not to mention the entire nation Israel. Grace, however, insists that forgiveness is available for everyone.

> *These sins would then be dropped into the deepest sea and a sign posted on the shore: "No fishing!"*

As a child I was encouraged to believe that repentance and faith in the blood of Jesus would separate me from my past sins as far as east is from west. These sins would then be dropped into the deepest sea and a sign posted on the shore: "No fishing!" Although I did not fully understand that for some years, I both believe and preach it now. It is good news. Furthermore, grace not only provides a fresh start, a new beginning, but grace also renews the perfect will of God. This is so important that it needs to be illustrated separately.

Renewing the Perfect Will of God

For many years I believed that once I sinned as a Christian, I would never be able to fulfill God's perfect will for my life. Oh, despair! One of the biggest revelations that I had had as a Christian is the realization that even the perfect will of God is constantly being updated.

I recall counseling a couple struggling with a troubled marriage. Both were Christians, and try as they may, the marriage still broke. It happens. Several years later the man phoned me and almost before I could say "Hello," blurted out: "It had to be God's perfect will for me and my former wife to be reconciled, right?"

Collecting myself as quickly as possible, I replied: "Yes, as far as I can tell."

He then sobbed and, almost whispering, added: "She just remarried, and I now see that reconciliation is never going to happen, and since I can no longer fulfill God's perfect will for my life, I am going to commit suicide. I simply cannot live with God's second best."

Instantly, I shouted, "Whoa! Wait just a minute; I've got good news. I'll be over in ten minutes." Arriving in eight, this is what I told him.

"Even the perfect will of God is constantly being updated. If God wants you to go to New York and you go to Los Angeles, then God has a perfect will for your return from Los Angeles. That is grace. Again, although sin has its consequences, the absolute perfect will of God is constantly being refreshed and renewed. Let me give you a hypothetical situation.

"Let's say that you know beyond doubt that God wants you to go to the airport and travel to some far away place until God tells you to return. You say, 'No, God! I love you with all my heart; but I'm just too busy. I have a new spouse; my father just died and I must attend to the funeral arrangements; and my new business simply cannot survive without me. Give me a raincheck.' Consequently, you live in the hell of disobedience for the next 24 hours (surely I am not the only one who knows what that means).

Then, 24 hours later, you say: 'OK, God! I give up. I am tired of living in the hell of disobedience. I do not know what you have in mind, but I am going to obey you.' At that point you go to the airport and get on a plane bound for your destination.

"The Law, in and of itself, says: 'OK, so you finally obeyed God. Well, for the rest of your sweet life you will be 24 hours behind the perfect will of God.' Grace, on the other hand, says: 'The moment you decide to obey God and board the plane (acting upon your conviction), you are at that moment where you would have been had you caught the plane 24 hours earlier.'"

I warned you at the outset of this study that grace sometimes bends the gray matter. It seems too good to be true.

I warned you at the outset of this study that grace sometimes bends the gray matter. It seems too good to be true. Some of you no doubt want chapter and verse. Here are a couple. Matthew 20:1-16, for example, tells the story of an estate owner who hired some of his workers in the morning (and they agreed upon a fair wage — let's say $20), some at midmorning, some at noon, some in the afternoon and some in the evening. At the end of the day he paid all of them $20, much to the dismay of those who had worked for so much longer. The owner's response? "I want to give the man who was hired last the same as I gave you. Don't I have the right to do what I want with my own money? Or are you envious because I am generous? 'So the last will be first, and the first will be last'" (vv. 15-16).[3]

Another example, of course, is the parable of the prodigal son (Luke 15:11-32). This time the father replies to the elder, "My son, you are always with me, and everything I have is yours. But we had to celebrate and be glad, because this brother of yours was dead and is alive again; he was lost and is found" (vv. 31-32).

So what is the moral of these stories? Again, sin obviously has its consequences. No one can deny that. Law, in and of itself, however, insists that those who disobey God (even for 24 hours) must settle for God's second best (sometimes referred to as the secondary or permissive will of God). Law would then remind them constantly, "You messed up and must pay for your sin." Grace, on the other hand, reminds us that even though we have sinned, and sin has its own immediate consequences, the perfect will of God is constantly being updated, refreshed and renewed, so that we can anticipate a future as full of potential as when we first believed.

Again, law, in and of itself, insists that those workers who were hired later in the day must not be paid as much as those hired at the beginning of the day. Grace simply expresses and then rejoices in the generosity of God. Once more, law, in and of itself, insists that the

> *Grace, on the other hand, reminds us that even though we have sinned, and sin has its own immediate consequences, the perfect will of God is constantly being updated, refreshed and renewed, so that we can anticipate a future as full of potential as when we first believed.*

prodigal be turned away (not welcomed), punished (not honored) or, at best, relegated to the role of servant (not restored to fellowship within the family). Grace portrays the mind of God as "love, joy, peace, patience, kindness, goodness, faithfulness, gentleness and self-control." Truly, "against such things there is no law" (Galatians 5:22-23).

Once more law, in and of itself, condemns without hope in the world. Grace affirms, "If we are still determined to fight sin in our lives, one minus does not negate all of the previous pluses." Law states that when we fall, we become defeated. Grace asks, "If I resist sin 10 times, why should one slip rule supreme?" Grace leads to repentance and renews its commitment to Jesus Christ so that we can move on ahead in spite of our temporary setbacks. Grace says, "You are not perfect, but sin is losing its constant threat, even its appeal. I am not defeated. I am yielding more and more to the Spirit of God." Grace exclaims, "Rejoice, God is still with you! Let God arise indeed."

Overcoming Sin in Persons and Systems

Up to this point we have addressed the issue of sin more on a personal level. Here and throughout the rest of our study we will necessarily broaden our understanding of sin (as well as righteousness) to include the corporate as well as the individual aspects of sin (as well as righteousness). Since sin is both personal and systemic, and since grace provides a theology for overcoming sin in persons and systems, here is a necessary word for both evangelical and humanist alike.

The evangelical must remember that grace (the power of the Holy Spirit) is given for ministry within *and* ministry without. If I do not develop the ability to see beyond myself, I will soon lose the ability to see within myself. Furthermore, grace is given both to individuals *and* in community for abolishing strongholds. Persons need community, and community needs connection with other communities if we are to storm the gates of hell. Spirit led unity is a mark of the new birth. In fact, a Spirit-filled community is a threat to the Enemy. We have got to watch each others backs.

The term "independent church" is an oxymoron. I just returned from Wisconsin. I saw thousands of geese flying in formation because they can fly 70 percent faster in formation than on their own.

They also swap leadership, honk to encourage each other, and if one drops out its mate (for life) drops out with it and remains with it until it recovers or dies. The church is community attached to community, determined to take the world by the scruff and shake the mischief out of it. Such a mountain of a task but the mind of Christ says that we had best take mountain-moving seriously.

I have always liked a quotation from Karl Barth's *Dogmatics in Outline*:

> Where the life of the Church is exhausted in self-serving, it smacks of death; the decisive thing has been forgotten, that is lived only in the exercise of what we called the Church's service as ambassador, proclamation, *kerygma*. A Church that recognizes its commission will neither desire nor be able to petrify in any of its functions, to be the Church for its own sake. There is the "Christ-believing group"; but this group is sent out: "Go and preach the gospel!" It does not say, "Go and celebrate services!" "Go and edify yourselves with the sermon!" "Go and celebrate the Sacraments!" "Go and present yourselves in a liturgy, which perhaps repeats the heavenly liturgy!" "Go and devise a theology which may gloriously unfold like the *Summa* of St. Thomas!" Of course, there is nothing to forbid all this; there may exist very good cause to do it all; but nothing, nothing at all for its own sake!

Evangelicals, take note, lest we (like the Pharisees) get caught criticizing Jesus for healing on the Sabbath. Barth was right. The church must always be inseparably linked with kingdom issues. I have always thought it interesting that Jesus challenges Peter with these words in Matthew 16:18-19: "On this rock I will build *my* church, the gates of Hades will not overcome it. I will give *you* the keys of the kingdom of heaven . . . (italics mine)." It seems as if Jesus were saying: "*I* will look after the Church (her organization and structure, even her spirituality); *you* get on with the business of the kingdom" (that is, doing the things that the Church has been called to do).

But haven't we reversed the roles? Our lack of love and obedience betray us. In effect, we have said, "Jesus, *we* will take care of the Church; *you* take care of the business of the kingdom." God has not so ordained the body of Jesus Christ. God is going to use us or God is not going to establish God's kingdom, at least in this generation. Oh, God could get along without us (make no mistake about that), but has chosen not to. God will work through us or God will return in all of God's glory to claim God's own if but out of the rubble.

Not surprisingly, in the very next passage Jesus reintroduces his favorite theme: "For whoever wants to save his life will lose it, but whoever loses his life for me will find it" (Matthew 16:25). We must not be led astray. We must not be discouraged.

Every sin manifest in the individual is manifest in society as a whole and God will surely hold us accountable if we as a church do not speak a prophetic word regarding a whole host of relevant issues, issues as personal as sexual immorality and as social as peace and justice. The next two chapters will attempt to spell this out in some detail.

> *Why are so many champions of such worthy causes giving up?*

Humanist, remember that grace must empower within before we can minister without. Too often our bankruptcy is our self-sufficiency. If I do not develop the ability to see within myself, I will soon lose the ability to see beyond myself. A few years ago I found myself weeping as I was reading the newspaper. Abbie Hoffman died. He had supposedly taken his own life. I said to myself: "He shouldn't have done that. He bailed out!" I know, Abbie Hoffman was a druggie and spent time in jail, but during my formative years he almost single-handedly stood in the gap against some fairly basic inhuman abuses. Then, within months, I read where Mitch Snyder, the so-called "apostle to the homeless," had hanged himself. Why? Why are so many champions of such worthy causes giving up? Then it hit me. The infinite power of the Holy Spirit had not been tapped.

In my earlier years I came out of the "hippie" movement. I was never a hippie (if only because no self-respecting hippie would claim me), but I did identify with many of their causes. I am now at the age when I go back to high school and college reunions (25 and 30 years). I am always a bit disappointed when I see almost all of my old hippie friends in three-piece suits having (in most cases) sold out to the system. I am the only one doing now what I was doing then. As we talk, the problem quicky surfaces. They simply burned out. Justice issues without the empowerment of the Holy Spirit tend to wear us down, usually within two or three years.

Only the Church of Jesus Christ is equipped to wage war against the principalities and powers of this present darkness. Paul writes,

> ... though we live in the world, we do not wage war as the world does. The weapons we fight with are not the weapons of the world. On the contrary, they [the weapons of God's people, the Church] have divine power to demolish strongholds (2 Corinthians 10:3-4).

The Church may not seem like much at times but she is all we have. Luther says it bluntly: "The Church is like Noah's Ark. If it wasn't for the storm on the outside, the stench on the inside would make me jump overboard."

Sanctifying grace overcomes sin in persons and systems. This section will serve as an introduction for the two chapters following. The gospel is both personal and social — two sides of the same coin. The church can never afford (as we are so prone to do) to pit one against the other. Surely the opposite of personal is not social, but impersonal; and the opposite of social is not personal, but antisocial. Again, the theology of law and grace is the theology of a church that is empowered by the Holy Spirit, dead serious about personal holiness, sensitized to human need and thoroughly offended by sin that is both individual and systemic.

Review

Sanctifying grace is the power of the Holy Spirit, cleansing, purifying and then setting us aside for kingdom ministry. It is the law of the Spirit of life setting us free from the law of sin and death. It is a fresh start, a new beginning so that we are truly forgiven and empowered to overcome sin in persons and systems.

Sanctifying grace creates a vision for individual and church, reminding them that the perfect will of God is constantly being updated so that we can anticipate (no matter what we might have done) as vital a ministry now as when we first believed.

Sanctifying grace renews our first love. Evangelical and humanist alike, take heed. The gospel of Jesus Christ is the good news that we are saved by grace through faith but that we are judged by our works. Salvation nurtures the roots; judgment inspects the inevitable fruit. Such balance! That is precisely what the fruit and gifts of the Holy Spirit are all about.

Study Questions:

1. What is sanctifying grace?
2. Can you contrast the law of sin and death with the law of the Spirit of life?
3. How does grace renew the perfect will of God?
4. What are our weapons of "divine power" for demolishing strongholds?
5. What is the fruit of sanctifying grace, personally and corporately?

Notes

[1]Wesley's *Works*, Vol. 1, pp. 103f.

[2]The image "body of death" here is probably taken from a first-century mode of execution where the condemned is bound mouth-to-mouth to a cadaver until death is achieved from inhaling the poisonous gases from within the cadaver itself or by asphyxiation.

[3]The concept of "last and first" is the one principle that Jesus emphasizes most throughout his ministry.

Luke 10:25-29   *1 Corinthians 13*
John 13:34-35   *2 Corinthians 4:18*
Romans 5:5; 8:16;   *1 John 4:7-8, 19*
13:8-10

*The fruit of the Spirit is love
but love has characteristics
such as joy, peace, patience,
kindness, goodness,
faithfulness, gentleness, and
self-control (Galatians 5:22-
23). This is the only
unmistakable mark of the
Spirit-filled life.*

1. Love is the unmistakable fruit of the Spirit.
2. To know God loves us enables us to love ourslves and our neighbors.
3. Assurance is also a fruit of the Spirit.

CHAPTER
10

For John Wesley the heart of Christianity could be captured by one word — love. He had a pretty good precedent for this. Jesus said, "A new command I give you:

The Fruit
of the Spirit
is Love

Love one another. As I have loved you, so you must love one another. By this all men will know that you are my disciples, if you love one another" (John 13:34-35).[1]

The apostle Paul quickly follows suit:

Let no debt remain outstanding, except the continuing debt to love one another, for he who loves his fellowman has fulfilled the law. The commandments . . . are summed up in this one rule: 'Love your neighbor as yourself.' Love does no harm to its neighbor. Therefore love is the fulfillment of the law" (Romans 13:8-10).

Add to these the words of the apostle John (1 John 4:7-8), "Dear friends, let us love one another, for love comes from God. Everyone who loves has been born of God and knows God. Whoever does not love does not know

God, because God is love," and the case is well established.

Obviously, all Christians must love, but how? What is the role of the Holy Spirit (sanctifying grace) in all of this? Furthermore, what does it really mean to love my neighbor as myself? Finally, a brief word about a doctrine of assurance as related to the fruit of the Holy Spirit will be included.

The Role of the Holy Spirit / Grace in Love

We have already established that sanctification simply refers to what sanctifying grace does — sin is rooted out, the fruit and gifts of the Spirit are given to the believer. We have already discussed the process of being saved from sin. Now we need to look closely at the fruit and gifts. This chapter examines the fruit. Our next chapter will examine the gifts.

It is fairly common knowledge that Wesley spoke of perfection in terms of pure love (see Chapter 12). I have already stated the importance of being "in Christ Jesus" as the key for exchanging the law as sin and death for the law as the Spirit of life. To be in Christ Jesus is to place our faith and trust in him alone. "By grace through faith," therefore, means that grace is appropriated or put to work through faith. Wesley states

> Faith, then, was originally designed of God to re-establish the law of love . . . . It is the grand means of restoring that holy love wherein man was originally created. It follows, that although faith is of no value in itself (as neither is any other means whatsoever), yet as it leads to that end, the establishing anew of the law of love in hearts; and as, in the present state of things, it is the only means under heaven for effecting it; it is on that account an unspeakable blessing to man, and of unspeakable value before God.

Let me illustrate just how practical this is for ministry for clergy and laity alike. I keep telling my students that they will enjoy their ministry to the precise degree that they love people and believe God's word. They sometimes respond, "Yes, but some people are just impossible to love."

True enough, if left to our own devices, but with God all things are possible. In our discussion of the new birth we mentioned that when the Holy Spirit comes into our lives two things occur (more or less) as inevitable fruit. The first is "hope does not disappoint us, because God has poured out his love into our hearts by the Holy Spirit, whom he has given us" (Romans 5:5). The second is "the Spirit himself testifies with our spirit that we are God's children" (Romans 8:16). Love and assurance, therefore, seem concomitant with the work of the Spirit. Let's focus first of all upon love.

Again, the Holy Spirit enables us to see others as God sees them, as we see our own children. When you can see me as you see your own children, I am so much easier to love. Furthermore, if we are resisting Spirit-assisted love, then our lack of love soon becomes apparent.

All of us are incredible communicators. We are such good communicators that if we tell people that we love them and do not mean it they usually smoke us out on the spot. If you do not love me you will find a way to communicate it, like it or not. I am such a good communicator that my wife can tell the mood I am in simply by the way I drive my automobile into the driveway. Although I frequently deny it (such futility), she is usually right. Knowing that fact, how do we love people so that when we tell them that we love them our words ring true. Quite simply, we open our lives afresh to the indwelling

All of us are incredible communicators. We are such good communicators that if we tell people that we love them and do not mean it they usually smoke us out on the spot.

power of the Holy Spirit by repenting of our inability to love and renewing our faith in Jesus Christ. When the Holy Spirit comes into our lives the whole world looks different.

I recall vividly the morning after my own conversion experience on the fifth floor of a fraternity house at Duke University. Nothing was the same. I wanted to hug and kiss everything that wiggled. I, quite literally, fell in love with all of God's creation. Even those who had previously been impossible to love began to reveal parts of their personality that I could respond to positively. Although I obviously did not love some of the things that they did, I could tell them that I loved them without sounding phony. I know, this sounds far too simplistic so let's spell out some of the necessary theology.

How Can I Love My Neighbor as Myself?

Again, Wesley writes,

> What adds a still greater sweetness, even to labor and pain, is the Christian "love of our neighbor." When they "love their neighbor," that is, every soul of man, "as themselves," as their own souls; when "the love of Christ constrains" them to love one another, "even as he loved us"; when, as he "tasted death for every man," so they are "ready to lay down their life for their brethren"; what prospect of danger will then be able to fright them from their "labor of love?"[2]

Throughout his works Wesley insisted that Christians must love their neighbors as themselves. As is so often the case, this raises an issue behind the issue. How does one love oneself (at least in the sense that is healthy and properly directed)? The answer should be fairly obvious. We love ourselves to the degree that we know ourselves to be loved by God.

God Loves Me First

It is interesting (if not tragic) that frequently our first sin (the sin behind all other sins) is our inability to believe that God loves us. The scenario goes something like this: One of the most basic principles in Christian theology is that if I do not believe that God loves me, then I do not love myself. If I do not love myself, then I love no one else and my motivation for overcoming the sin that oppresses my neighbor is sorely lacking, if not dead altogether.

I confess that I was a Christian for 15 years before I could really believe that God loved me. Thinking this extremely odd, imagine my surprise when I discovered that this is all too common. So what is the problem?

For starters, we are told that 40 percent of us were abused either sexually or physically as children. Although I was never abused as a child, I can certainly understand how difficult it might be for those who were to believe in a loving God. Just last week I heard myself saying from the pulpit of a church, "If you are presently abusing your children I pray to God that one of two things happens immediately. Either you get help or you go to jail!" What we are learning these days about the horrible impact of child abuse on God awareness and even religious understanding in general should break our hearts.

Many of my students have become so sensitized to gender (especially male imagery), not just because of inclusiveness issues, but because of patterns of abuse, that learning is severely hampered if I do not make an honest attempt to avoid all male (or female) exclusive references unless cited as a part of a direct quotation. For that reason I try to use words that heal. If I truly care about people, how could I do less in the name of love? Believe me, what I gain is far greater than what I might possibly lose. As important as theology is, there comes a time when we best stop doing theology and start doing ministry.

Just last week I heard myself saying from the pulpit of a church, "If you are presently abusing your children I pray to God that one of two things happens immediately. Either you get help or you go to jail!"

There are, of course, other reasons why some of us have a difficult time believing that God loves us. Perfectionists and legalists abound. One of the Enemy's greatest ploys is to convince the serious-minded seeker that he or she can never quite measure up. More will be said about this in our last chapter but, for now, know that the problem is considerable. If this is your burden, then you are not alone.

I recall going jogging one day, feeling depressed, wondering whether or not God still loved me, thinking probably not. God then spoke to me by giving me an insight that was far bigger than I was. The gist of what God was saying went something like this: "Tuttle, don't you know why I love you? I don't love you because I am a God of love, though I am; and I don't love you because that is what I do best, though it is; and I don't love you because I'm supposed to, though I am. The reason I love you is, there's just something about you that flat out turns me on." Wow! I was healed in an instant. My name was no longer Legion. I finished that run with a rush.

I finally realized that there was actually something about me that God liked. Even now I hesitate to tell you that story (though I have told it many times before) since it apparently lacks humility. None of us likes to get caught with our pride hanging out. Listen to the point, however. There is no cause for pride. God simply affirmed who I am as a part of God's good creation. "We love because God first loved us," (1 John 4:19). Indeed!

Loving myself

So, God loves me for who I am. Surely, the moral is this: God responds to something within me (messed up as I am at times), and if I am good enough for God to love, I ought to be good enough for you. What do you think of that? I'll tell you something else. If *you* are good enough for God to love, you are good enough for those around you. Even more important, if you are good enough for God to love, you ought to be good enough for *yourself!*

> *If you are good enough for God to love, you ought to be good enough for* yourself!

Again, the principle is this: If I do not know that God loves me, I do not love myself. If I do not love myself, I do not love anyone. The solution? Am I willing for God to take from me my inability to believe that God loves me (the essence of repentance) by renewing my faith and trust in Jesus Christ (the essence of justification) and receiving the gift of salvation by the power of the Holy Spirit (the essence of the new birth), so that the next time I am tempted to believe that God does not love me, my first inclination will be to resist it (the essence of sanctification)?

Loving My Neighbor

To state the above principle positively: "If I know that God loves me, I can love myself. If I can love myself, I can love others." In his sermon, "On Family Religion," Wesley insists that serving God is first of all the service of faith which immediately produces love.

> As soon as he believes, he loves God, which is another
> thing implied in "serving the Lord." "We love him be-
> cause he first loves us"; of which faith is the evidence . . . .
> If any man truly love God, he cannot but love his brother
> also. Gratitude to our Creator will surely produce benevo-
> lence to our fellow-creatures. If we love Him, we cannot
> but love one another, as Christ loved us. We feel our souls
> enlarged in love toward every child of man.[3]

Jesus, of course, also calls us to love our neighbor as we love ourselves.

How many of us have been tempted to ask (along with the
"expert in the law" in Luke 10:25-29), "Who is my neighbor?" In
reaction to those who might forget their neighbor by considering a
wholly contemplative life within some far-away cloister Wesley writes:

> Directly opposite to this is the gospel of Christ. Solitary
> religion is not to be found there. "Holy Solitaries" is a
> phrase no more consistent with the gospel than holy adul-
> terers [speaking of oxymorons]. The gospel of Christ knows
> of no religion, but social; no holiness but social holiness.
> "Faith working by love" is the length and breadth and
> depth and height of Christian perfection . . . . And in truth,
> whosoever loveth his brethren, not in word only, but as
> Christ loved him, cannot but be "zealous of good works."
> He feels in his soul a burning, restless desire of spending
> and being spent.[4]

Clearly, my neighbor is anyone in need. To be loved by God is to
experience a burning desire to love others in word *and* deed. Let's be
more specific.

If you were to read straight through the Bible from Genesis to
Revelation, two great sins keep appearing and reappearing — self-
reliance and oppressing the poor. God's judgment lies heavily upon
those who live as if there were no God. Humanism is without doubt
one of the greatest sins as it first boasts of its own power, and then
wallows in its own impotence. But that has been spoken of before.
God's judgment is equally harsh upon those who oppress the poor.

Recently I was teaching and preaching in Korea. For the last 20 years the church has been growing faster in Korea than in any other place in the world. Why? It appears to me that there are at least four reasons. First, the Koreans know how to pray. They had me up at 4:00 a.m. attending a daily prayer meeting held seven mornings a week. When I arrived at the church, more than 5,000 people had gotten there ahead of me. They had to put chairs in the aisles while we prayed for two hours. Second, the Koreans know how to believe God for the increase. Their faith is phenomenal. Third, the Koreans know how to disciple their converts. Nothing is left to chance. Every member must be in covenant with some small group. Finally, the Korean Church has throughout its 100-year history always identified with the oppressed.

> *Within the Asian culture, to identify with the oppressor is to lose face.*

Within the Asian culture, to identify with the oppressor is to lose face. It is true of the Korean "crown prince" who must now live in Japan, and it is true of the American military who must barricade its embassy. Both were caught identifying with the oppressor. I told my students that the revival in Korea could well last more than one generation (they usually do not) if they continue to pray, believe, disciple and identify with the oppressed.

John Wesley insisted that he could keep his Methodists sane (free from the excesses of enthusiasm), but he could not keep them from becoming rich and respectable. He writes,

> What a hinderance are riches to the very first fruit of faith,—namely, the love of God! . . . . Riches are equally a hinderance to the loving our neighbour as ourselves; that is, to the loving all mankind as Christ loved us. A rich man may indeed love them that are of his own party, or his own opinion. He may love them that love him . . . . But he cannot have pure, disinterested goodwill to every child of man. This can only spring from the love of God, which his great possessions expelled from his soul.[5]

How easy to lose our sensitivity to the poor. Wesley was always fearful of doing just that. He gives this advice to a member of the Society:

> Go and see the poor and sick in their own poor little hovels. Take up your cross, woman! Remember the faith! Jesus went before you, and will go with you. Put off the gentlewoman . . . . I have found some of the uneducated poor who have exquisite taste and sentiment; and many, very many, of the rich who have scarcely any at all. But I do not speak of this: I want you to converse more, abundantly more, with the poorest of the people, who, if they have not taste, have souls, which you may forward in their way to heaven. And they have (many of them) faith, and the love of God, in a larger measure than any persons I know.[6]

Every time I am confronted by poverty I want to sell all that I own and give it to the poor. Alas, the conviction always wears off. This past year I decided if I would not sell all, I could at least find some "kingdom investments" that would directly benefit those most in need. Perhaps naively, I wanted a first-hand look. I took a couple of students into Third World countries, determined never to pass a beggar without touching, giving money, and speaking a word for God. We made it through China and parts of southeast Asia without abandoning our cause. We learned a great deal. It would take a separate book to describe the adventure. India, however, overwhelmed us.

I took a couple of students into Third World countries, determined never to pass a beggar without touching, giving money, and speaking a word for God.

With hundreds clinging to us almost at once, I could not fulfill my promise to touch, give and speak to each one individually. I became frustrated and depressed. We ended up in Calcutta, observing the work of Mother Teresa, dressing the sores in a leprosarium and holding the helpless in a "home for the dying."

After returning home (my wife threatening to have me dusted

and dipped), I realized that although I was not able to fulfill my vow of reaching out to each one individually, I did have names and addresses of places where I was certain that money sent would be money well spent. If you are looking for a good "Kingdom investment," I can give you an address where $10 a month provides food and shelter for an orphan or $25 a month feeds a family of three. A couple of thousand dollars from a church school class can build an entire church where local pastors can teach and preach, feed and clothe, and all in the name of Jesus.

As I consider the rest of the world I realize that I am disgustingly wealthy. Paul warns in 1 Timothy 4:2 that the conscience can become seared as with a hot iron. Oh, to remain sensitive to human need. Jesus talks more about money than he does about prayer because he knew that it was difficult to maintain a God-awareness and have lots of money. It has something to do with serving two masters and a camel walking through the eye of a needle. Our dogs are fatter than the world's children. None of us is exempt from the temptation not to care. Little wonder Jesus uses the story of the good Samaritan to illustrate love for one's neighbor. God help me lest I become a priest or Levite bypassing suffering humanity on some Jericho road.

> *Jesus talks more about money than he does about prayer because he knew that it was difficult to maintain a God awareness and have lots of money.*

Poverty, oppression and need are not only abroad, but at home. As a nation I personally believe that America has a particular responsibility to share some of its incredible resources with the underdeveloped countries around the world, but we must not become blind to those within our own immediate reach. Jesus never went out of his way to help anyone. He never had time. He was so sensitized to those in front of him that it was all that he could do to minister to those within a 60-mile radius of where he lived.

Recently an evaluation was distributed by the ruling body of a mainline denomination to churches being served by recent seminary graduates. These first and second year pastors were to be evaluated in 17 different areas of ministry. The result was interesting. All of them received predominantly negative marks in every category but one. The only category to receive consistently high marks was funerals (one of the things that we frequently do not teach in seminary). In other words, grief work was done carefully and effectively. Why?

It occurred to me that many of our seminary graduates enter the local church oblivious to the needs in front of them. We are bent on "consciousness raising" for needs *out there*. The only time many of these new pastors are aware of needs within their own congregations is when someone dies. Then they become loving and vulnerable and they do ministry well.

Solomon writes, "It is better to go to a house of mourning than to go to a house of feasting . . ." (Ecclesiastes 7:2). The late Malcolm Muggeridge claimed that "death and dying wonderfully concentrate the mind." The longer I live the more I am convinced that incredible pain is all around us. We do not have to wait until someone dies to score high marks on loving and caring. Psychologist Howard Clinebell convinces us that everyone grieves. We grieve over matters as unrelated as the loss of hair to the loss of a mate.

If Galatians 5:22 identifies the fruit of the Spirit, then surely 1 Corinthians 13 spells it out:

> Love is patient, love is kind. It does not envy, it does not boast, it is not proud. It is not rude, it is not self-seeking, it is not easily angered, it keeps no record of wrongs. Love does not delight in evil but rejoices with the truth. It always protects, always trusts, always hopes, always perseveres (vv. 4-7).

E. Stanley Jones once told me that Paul in writing these words dipped his pen in the blood of his broken heart and set pain to music. Love overcomes sin.

For those who love, sin is no longer what it is cracked up to be.

The only time many of these new pastors are aware of needs within their own congregations is when someone dies.

Sin maims and separates. Love binds and heals. Love feeds the hungry, clothes the naked and visits the sick and imprisoned. Love speaks a timely word of good news about the grace or power available through faith in Jesus Christ. Not that we love *in order to* evangelize. We evangelize *because* we love. There is a difference. One smacks of manipulation. The other rings true. Let me illustrate.

A student of mine recently turned in this case study for a course in evangelism. "I was riding in an automobile with an elderly neighbor behind the wheel. There was a minor accident. The young driver of the other car jumped out and began cursing my neighbor rudely. My neighbor became so confused that I simply said to him, 'Go on home and let me handle it.' I then suggested that the young man and I go to the nearby home of the young man to work out the damages that were assessed (somewhat liberally) at $300.

> *Not that we love* in order *to evangelize. We evangelize* because *we love.*

"The young man and his mother were astonished to see me immediately write out a check (which I could ill afford) for that amount. They had assumed that the old man and I were related, and when they discovered that I was just a friend of someone who needed assistance, they were impressed, if not a bit ashamed. Coffee was then served and it was soon revealed that the young man and his mother were Christians without a church home. Since I was serving a church in the neighborhood an invitation to attend was extended."

The closing remarks of the case study went something like this, "They come to church every Sunday and I visit them regularly at home." My own comments following were, "Perhaps the best $300 you'll ever spend. God will give it back, pressed down, shaken together, running over. You can never outgive God!"

Paul makes an important observation in 2 Corinthians 4:18, " . . . what is seen is temporary, but what is unseen is eternal." One might well translate that: "the only things eternal are unseen." Again, there is far more reality beyond the senses than within the senses. The only way to take it with you is to give it away. You will never see a hearse with a "U-haul" trailer behind it.

Jesus had a way of reversing the world's standards. Reduce his gospel to one great passion and it would have to be: "Give up your life for my sake and gain it." The only way to be first is to be last. The only way to be great is to be a servant. Mark's gospel highlights Christ as "servant" as his predominant theme. Not surprisingly, Peter (who was perhaps Mark's primary source) in his sermon recorded in Acts 3 speaks of Jesus as "servant." The fruit of the Spirit is love seeking to serve.

Earlier I mentioned a journalist friend bored with the world's standards. He was concerned with issues simply too big for him to engage on his own. He was a frustrated ecologist concerned about water and the ozone. He was a feminist concerned with equal rights and pornography. He was a pacifist concerned with war and nuclear build-up (40 times the amount of fire power already on line to destroy completely planet earth). He was a socialist concerned with equality and feeding the hungry. Most of all, he was an agnostic because the Christian church was apparently no more than slightly annoyed with any of these problems.

OK, Christian, what about racism, sexism, abortion, population control, crime, drugs, poverty, housing and a whole host of other concerns where Jesus no doubt dwells among the "least of these brothers [and sisters] of mine" (Matthew 25:31-46)? If love is the inevitable fruit of the Spirit, then the apostle John is right: "Whoever does not love does not know God" (I John 4:8). That is the downside. Listen to the upside: "God is not unjust; he will not forget your work and the love you have shown him as you have helped his people and continue to help them" (Hebrews 6:10).

God expects the Church to deal with sin in persons and systems. The fruit of the Spirit motivates us to act. The gifts of the Spirit empower us to overcome. As the song says, "Just keep praising God, never sound retreat." Before we address the important chapter on gifts, however, a brief word concerning assurance needs to be spoken.

Assurance and the Fruit of the Spirit

Since the Spirit promises not only to shed God's love abroad in our hearts (Rom. 5:5) but promises also to bear witness with our spirits that we are children of God (Rom. 8:16), many see assurance as an inevitable fruit of the Spirit as well. Wesley early in his ministry agreed. Every Christian must necessarily know that they are in right relationship with God. In 1747 (less than 10 years into the Revival), however, he changed this opinion. After 1747 Wesley taught that an assurance of salvation was the "common privilege," not necessarily the inevitable proof of acceptance with God.

The reason for this shift will become more apparent in the next chapter. For now, Wesley began to associate his doctrine of assurance with the gift of faith. Since all gifts are for the church but not necessarily for the individual, Wesley was forced to struggle with the obvious inconsistency.

Review

The fruit of the Spirit is love. Although love has fruits (or characteristics) of its own (joy, peace, patience, kindness, goodness, faithfulness, gentleness and self-control [Galatians 5:22-23]), love itself is the lowest common denominator for all that is Christian. The Holy Spirit enables us to see others as God sees them. Furthermore, for Christians, to know that God loves us is to love ourselves and to love ourselves is to love others. Loving others is the motivation behind all of our attempts at ministry. "And now these three remain: faith, hope and love. But the greatest of these is love" (1 Corinthians 13:13). Paul's next words introducing the next chapter: "Follow the way of love and eagerly desire spiritual gifts" (1 Corinthians 14:1), will introduce our next chapter as well.

Study Questions:

1. What is the fruit of the Spirit?
2. What is the role of the Holy Spirit/grace in love?
3. Do I know that God loves me so that I can love myself and others?
4. What are two of the greatest sins in the Bible?
5. How does the fruit of the Spirit speak to those sins?

Notes

[1]Remember that these are the opening words of the "Farewell Discourse" where Jesus outlines the work of the Holy Spirit/grace.

[2]Wesley's *Works*, Vol. 6, p. 160.

[3]Wesley's *Works*, Vol. 7, p. 78.

[4]Wesley's *Works*, Vol. 14, p. 321.

[5]Wesley's *Works*, Vol. 7, p. 216.

[6]Wesley's *Works*, Vol. 12, pp. 300f.

Romans 12:3-8 *Ephesians 4:1-13*
1 Corinthians 12 *1 Peter 4:7-11*

*The gifts of the Holy Spirit
are those supernatural
abilities given by the Holy
Spirit enabling Christians to
minister effectively within
their own spheres of
influence. To be effective the
gifts must be manifested
within the context of the
fruit.*

1. The range and scope of the gifts of the Holy Spirit are discussed.

2. The gifts of the Spirit enable the various parts of the body of Christ (the church) to minister effectively within their own spheres of influence.

3. Since every Christian's sphere of influence is different then their spiritual gifts will be different as well.

CHAPTER
11

Toward the end of the last chapter we quoted 1 Peter 4:8: "Above all, love each other deeply, because love covers over a multitude of sins." Here is the rest of that

The Gifts
of the Holy Spirit:
Readiness for Ministry

passage: "Offer hospitality to one another without grumbling. Each one should use whatever gift he has received to serve others, faithfully administering God's grace in its various forms" (vv. 9f.).

Love rules the gifts. If you have the kind of mentality that must choose between fruit and gifts (and apparently some do), then by all means choose the fruit:

> If I speak in the tongues of men and of angels, but have no love, I am only a resounding gong or a clanging cymbal. If I have the gift of prophecy and can fathom all mysteries and all knowledge, and if I have a faith that can move mountains, but have not love, I am nothing (1 Cor. 13:1f.).

As for me, however, I will not be satisfied until the fruit *and* the gifts are fully at work in the church. Although loves rules supreme the church will never be the church that God intends for her to be without all of the Spirit's gifts freely operating within her fellowship.

The Source of the Gifts

First of all, the gifts of the Holy Spirit have a *supernatural* origin. They are generally not "talents" that can be generated by practice and determination. The gifts of the Holy Spirit enable us to function beyond our own natural ability. This is not to disparage of God-given talents. Certainly talents under an anointing from the Holy Spirit can become gifts. My wife plays the piano. She tells me that sometimes within a worship setting her talent for playing the piano becomes greater than her ability. Although she does not suddenly play like Mozart, an anointing from God can turn an ordinary talent into an extraordinary gift.

I have had similar experiences preaching. You have no idea how boring seminary professors can be. There have been times when struggling out of my own spirit, half way through my sermon I have found myself thinking: "God, I am up here dying; I want to go home, now!" On the other hand, I have had other experiences where my ordinary talent for preaching has received an extraordinary anointing so that I could sense the Holy Spirit at work within the congregation.

Once more, let me reiterate. God is the supernatural source of spiritual gifts. The Apostle Paul writes,

> There are different kinds of gifts, but the same Spirit.
> There are different kinds of service, but the same Lord.
> There are different kinds of working of one and the same Spirit, and he gives them to each one, just as he determines" (1 Cor. 12:4-6, and 11).

The Definition and Scope of Spiritual Gifts

The gifts of the Holy Spirit are different kinds of ministries given by God to the Church, the body of Jesus Christ, and manifested through her individual parts so that every Christian can be prepared, fully equipped, and ready for ministry. Again, Paul writes:

"Now about spiritual gifts, brothers, I do not want you to be ignorant" (1 Cor. 12:1). The Greek word for spiritual gifts here is *pneumatikon*, perhaps best translated as "spirituals" or "things spiritual." Later on in that same passage (quoted in the previous paragraph), the term for gifts is *charismata*, which builds on *pneumatikon*, but focuses upon specific gifts. Paul then lists nine gifts related to the various aspects of ministry within the church:

> . . . to each one the manifestation of the Spirit is given for the common good. To one there is given through the Spirit the message of wisdom, to another the message of knowledge by means of the same Spirit, to another faith by the same Spirit, to another gifts of healing by that one Spirit, to another miraculous powers, to another prophecy, to another distinguishing between spirits, to another speaking in different kinds of tongues, and to still another the interpretation of tongues (1 Cor. 12:7-10).

Obviously, some of these gifts relate to the intellect, like wisdom, knowledge and discernment (sometimes referred to as the "intuitive" gifts). Others refer to the miraculous, such as faith, healing and the working of miracles (sometimes called the "power" gifts). Still others relate to the spoken word, like prophecy, tongues and interpreting tongues (sometimes referred to as the "prophetic" gifts).

Furthermore, additional New Testament passages (Rom. 12, Eph. 4, and I Peter 4, for example) list at least 19 other gifts (prophecy being the only gift common to all four passages). No list, however, is intended to be definitive. These gifts (often referred to as "classical" or "pentecostal") simply depict the range or scope of the Spirit's gifts. There are hundreds of gifts, different one's of which are suited to each body part making that particular body part indispensable to the whole. Let me explain.

The Use of the Spirit's Gifts

All of the passages that relate to spiritual gifts have at least one thing in common — the gifts are always seen within the context of the body. All gifts are given to the church, but not necessarily to the individual. Individuals receive only those gifts appropriate for their particular sphere of influence.

Each of us has a sphere of influence where only we can minister most effectively. You come into contact with people every day that I could not relate to nearly as effectively as you can. Another basic principle of law and grace is that although God will hold us accountable for our faithfulness to our own sphere, God has more invested in that sphere than we do. God not only loves us first; God is already at work within our sphere preparing people (remember prevenient grace) for our particular ministry.

We can be bold because God has gone before us and to be effective is simply to move into the mainstream of God's already intercession. Furthermore, God guarantees that whatever gifts are necessary to enable us to minister effectively within that sphere are available to us. Every Christian is gifted. Unfortunately, if not tragically, many are not aware of just how much is available.

The church must constantly remind and encourage every part of the body to exercise its gifts. Now wait! That is not to say that the church can make any one gift normative for the whole. That mistake has split many a church and in my opinion the Scripture expressly forbids that kind of interpretation (1 Cor. 12:29-31). In fact, if our spheres are different our gifts will be different. Since no two spheres are identical, no two Christians will have indentical gifts. That means that I do not have to covet your gift, and you do not have to covet mine.

> *Every Christian is gifted. Unfortunately, if not tragically, many are not aware of just how much is available.*

Equally important, I cannot lay a "trip" on you by insisting that you manifest my particular gift(s) and you cannot lay a "trip" on me by insisting that I manifest your particular gift(s). We can rejoice in each other's gifts. I have frequently said, "Messianic complexes die hard." Be grateful that no one body part has to carry the responsibility for all of the gifts of the Spirit.

Spiritual gifts are levelers. They insure that each body part is essential to the whole. Paul continues,

> The eye cannot say to the hand, "I don't need you!" And the head cannot say to the feet, "I don't need you!" On the

contrary, those parts of the body that seem to be weaker are *indispensable*, and the parts that we think are less honorable we treat with special modesty, while our presentable parts need no special treatment. But God has combined the members of the body and has given greater honor to the parts that lacked it, so that there should be no division in the body, but that its parts should have equal concern for each (1 Cor. 12:21-25, italics mine).

United Methodist minister and former basketball star Ed Beck tells a wonderful story. Just prior to the 1988 summer Olympics he visited the training center for the Olympic athletes in Colorado Springs where he lives. Thinking that he might find an illustration on the importance of community he was disappointed. These marvelous athletes were simply too competitive. Then the "Special Olympics" came to town. They were held at the Air Force Academy. Beck described the 100 yard dash.

> *Suddenly about 50 yards down the track one of the runners in the main pack fell.*

He said that as the gun went off some of the runners were fairly fast and immediately left the rest behind. Others were moving little better than a walk. Suddenly about 50 yards down the track one of the runners in the main pack fell. Immediately, the entire race stopped. Even those who were close to the finish line returned to their fallen friend and gathered around shouting: "Are you all right? Are you all right?" The one fallen responded: "No! I'm not all right; I hurt!" At that point a beautiful thing happened.

One of the runners knelt down, brushed off the scrape, kissed it and helped the injured runner to his feet. At that point they all held hands determined to restart the race from the middle of the track. As they looked back and forth at each other they all shouted: "Are you ready? Are you ready?" at which point the gun went off again and they all started to run but they forgot to let go of the hands of the one's next to them so they all finished the race together; and no one lost; and everyone won.

I like that. That is a powerful parable on the Church.

The gifts of the Holy Spirit mean that every body part is important. There are no exceptions. Sometimes I feel so inadequate. My weaknesses nearly paralyze me. Yet, when Paul complained of his "thorn in the flesh," God's reply was timeless: "My grace is sufficient for you, for my power is made perfect in weakness" (2 Cor. 12:9). In fact, weakness in the Bible is frequently not something to be overcome, it is the place where God dwells.

Again, the church must teach and encourage each of her body parts to exercise their particular gifts. No church should discourage the manifestation of gifts simply because some have exploited them. Paul took special pains to direct and correct so that no community would be without and no community would abuse the gifts of the Holy Spirit (1 Cor. 14). Do not be denied what God makes available for ministry. It is the difference between self-sufficient bankruptcy and frustration and God-sufficient power and fulfillment. Every Christian is a priest, whether lay or ordained. God's anointing is far more important that a bishop's.

The Reception of the Spirit's Gifts

Several important questions now come to mind. If God provides gifts to every part of the body in order for that part to fulfill its ministry effectively, how does one know which gifts are for whom and how does one then receive these all important gifts?

Which Gifts Are for Me?

It is my firm conviction that our natural spheres of influence usually determine the supernatural gifts that are necessary in order to fulfill our particular ministry. Let me illustrate.

If I live in a place where the majority of my colleagues and friends are not Christians, then I would expect that God might give me the gift of evangelism. If I have a heart for the sick, it seems logical to me that God might give me the gift of healing or mercy. If I live among the poor or oppressed, then God might well give me the gift of giving or service or even prophetic utterance.

Although this is an oversimplification and there are situations where God will gift a person for ministry outside of their immediate sphere, the principle still holds true — natural sphere usually determines supernatural gifts. My friend, Jim Buskirk, says: "If you want to know what your gifts are, go home and tackle something so big that you fall flat on your nose without God." There is a saying among distance runners: "The real race begins at that point in the race when you absolutely, positively, cannot take another step." There is a lesson there for the Church. God helps those who can no longer help themselves.

How Do I Receive the Gifts that I Need for Ministry?

Where and when do gifts surface? That is an important question. The answer is actually fairly straightforward: gifts surface within the context of ministry. In other words, gifts are given when I venture out in faith and obedience to fulfill whatever ministry God has placed upon my heart, believing that the necessary gifts will surface when the need arises.

Some years ago I was picked up at an airport and driven to a preaching engagement. En route, my driver blurted out, "I've just got to have more God"; to which I replied, "What are you doing with what you have already?"

His answer: "Nothing."

For the life of me I cannot understand the kind of "spirituality" that keeps asking God for more when it has not yet put to work what it already has. When I shared this with him, he responded, "You mean that I cannot receive more God in this meeting?"

I answered as lovingly but as honestly as I knew how: "Probably not. You have all the Holy Spirit you need for what miserable little bits of ministry that you have attached yourself to. Go home, repent, renew your faith and trust in Jesus Christ and then reach out and touch someone. Then watch the Spirit's power flow."

You will never follow a God impluse and regret it!

That man remembered that conversation and told me years later that that was a real turning point in his walk with God. I never cease to be amazed at what God can do with those willing to love and obey (two concepts forever linked in the Scriptures). *You will never follow a God impluse and regret it!* Remember, God has more invested in your ministry than you do.

Nearly a year ago I was preaching in a small southern town. Sunday noon I was dropped off at the airport after a dozen presentations in less than three days only to find that my flight had been cancelled. Although I was scheduled to preach that evening in Detroit, I was too tired to care. I flopped around the airport for a couple of hours on standby status, finally catching a flight for Atlanta. Arriving in Atlanta the only way to get me to Detroit that evening was on a flight in first class.

Although I am not accustomed to first class, I ran on the plane and crawled across a distinguished-looking gentleman who looked like he belonged in first class. I was so exhausted that I said nothing to him, and he said nothing to me.

My immediate response was, "God, he'll think I'm crazy!

The meal was served shortly after takeoff. Again, I do not know how God speaks to you, but God speaks to me by giving me insights that are bigger than I am. Half way through the main course I received this insight: "Tell the man next to you that if he will allow my Spirit to increase his vision for ministry he won't have to spend the next 20 years simply holding on to what he already has."

My immediate response was, "God, he'll think I'm crazy! I've not said 'boo' to him and he's not said 'boo' to me." Once again the same insight. After a third time, I prayed, "OK God, I give up. You open the door and I will speak the word."

Within seconds the piece of meat I was chewing became so tough that I could not swallow it. What do you do with a piece of meat that you cannot swallow when the napkins in first class are cloth, not paper? I then turned to my neighbor and said, "This meat is tough."

He smiled (actually, I think he winked) and said, "Yeah, I just gave up on that meat myself."

Feeling somewhat encouraged, I then asked him (for the life of me I do not know why), "Do you make an honest living?"

His immediate reply, "You know, I don't."

This candid response so surprised me that it caught me off guard. I blushed and asked, "Do we need to talk about that?"

Like a flash he answered, "I just saw you pray over your meal [which I do not remember doing but I am certain he would not have made that up] and I think we need to talk about that."

Within 15 minutes I felt that I could share with him the insight that I believed to be from God, but the moment I spoke the words, "If you will allow my Spirit to increase your vision for ministry, you will not have to spend the next twenty years simply holding on to what you already have," the man broke. He sobbed so that he could not speak. For the next few minutes I simply held him trying to console him thinking, "Help me God! What have I done?"

He sobbed so that he could not speak. For the next few minutes I simply held him trying to console him thinking, "Help me God! What have I done?"

As my friend began to recover, he told me this story: "I own a business in the Fortune 500. Just before you spoke to me I was about to make a decision that was better for profit than for people, and I asked God if God really cared, and if God really did care to show me. Within seconds you told me your meat was tough, and we began to get acquainted. When you spoke the words that you believed to be from God, I became so convicted that I had to confess, 'God I'm sorry and I promise you this: I'm not going to be an oppressor of people anymore!'" At that point the plane landed, but as we exited the man stayed with me.

As we approached the person waiting to rush me to a restless congregation (I was two hours late), my new friend took the man by the lapels of his jacket and said, "I've just had the most incredible experience of my life. I'm like the Ethiopian eunuch [Acts 8]. God prepared my heart to receive this man's message and I told God that I would testify to the first person I saw when I got off the plane and you are it. I was about to make a decision that was better for profit than for people and I want you to know that I am not going to be an oppressor of people anymore." With that he excused himself and disappeared in the crowd.

We still correspond and the story gets even better, but there is not time to tell it now. The point here is that the Spirit of God gifts us at the point of our obedience to God impluses. That experience was simply bigger than I am. God had delivered the man into my hands. If I had a bit more natural talent I might be able to take some of the credit myself, but since I am who I am, I can only give God the glory. That's the honest truth.

Gifts for the Church as Well as the Individual

The term "oppressor" in that last story is interesting in light of our earlier insistence that grace/Holy Spirit overcomes sin in persons and systems. Persons oppress persons but systems oppress the masses. Just as the Holy Spirit can gift the individual for overcoming sins against persons, the Holy Spirit can gift the Church for overcoming the sins against the masses. A Spirit-filled congregation can wield incredible power. The eighteenth-century Evangelical Revival, for example, literally changed the history of a nation.

In his sermon, "Marks of the New Birth," Wesley writes,

> An immediate and constant fruit of this faith whereby we are born of God, a fruit which can in no wise be separated from it, no, not for an hour, is the power over sins; — power over outward sin of every kind; over every evil word and work . . . . "[1]

Although Wesley was more of an Evangelist than a social reformer, his message of personal salvation to the disenchanted masses of the eighteenth century resulted in a social consciouness as well. For Wesley, conversion transcended both wealth and poverty by placing all persons in the same class — saved. The effect of this was (at least within the Methodist societies) that none had too much and none had too little.

I've always been rather intrigued with this letter written to John Wesley and included in his own journal:

> Sir, I was yesterday led to hear what God would say to me by your mouth. You exhorted us to "strive to enter at the straight gate." I am willing so to do. But I find one chief part of my striving must be, to feed the hungry, to clothe the naked, to instruct the ignorant, to visit the sick and such as are in prison, bound in misery and iron.

But if you purge out all who scorn such practices, or at least are not found in them, how many will remain in your society? I fear scarce enough to carry your body to the grave! Alas, how many, even among those who are called believers, have plenty of all the necessities of life, and yet complain of poverty! How many have houses and lands, or bags of money, and yet cannot find in their hearts to spare now and then to God's poor a little piece of gold! How many have linen in plenty, with three or four suits of clothes, and can see the poor go naked! They will change them away for painted clay, or let the moths devour them, before they will give them to cover the nakedness of their poor brethren, many of whose souls are clothed with glorious robes, though their bodies are covered with rags. Pray, Sir, tell these, you cannot believe they are Christians, unless they imitate Christ in doing good to all men, and hate covetousness, which is idolatry.[2]

Wesley answered: "I do tell them so: And I tell them it will be more tolerable in the day of judgment for Sodom and Gormorrah than for them."[3]

Although early Methodism was not exclusively a movement of the poor, most Methodists lived among the lower order of the laboring class. As pointed out by Tom Albin in a lecture entitled "Early Methodism and the Poor" delivered at a recent American Academy of Religion meeting:

Theologically, Methodism under the leadership of the Wesley brothers maintained a stress on the importance of the inner life, and at the same time insisted that an authentic spiritual life must find practical expression in outward actions to benefit the poor and needy. Methodism stood over against the more contemplative way of other mystic and Quietist options available during this period. And in contrast to the deistic and Trinitarian controversies that ravaged Dissent, for the most part Methodism was able to keep speculative theology subservient to the larger issues of love, obedience and humble service. In short, the Methodist Societies functioned like a lay religious order which enabled men and women to work out their own salvation, and at the same time maintain a socially redemptive involvement with the poor and vulnerable around them.

John Wesley wrote repeatedly that "'faith working by love' is the length and breadth and depth and height of Christian perfection. This commandment we have from Christ, that the one who loves God loves one's brother or sister also and that we manifest our love by doing good unto all people." For Wesley, conversion was two-sided (personal and social) indeed, a full gospel. Religious zeal and social enthusiasm went hand in hand as inseparable, indivisible, never to be divided, until Christ can be proved the fool and the Scriptures a lie. That was John Wesley's legacy to the people called Methodists: an incredible balance among issues frequently at odds with each other. May his tribe increase. Let's now look at some specific systems that have oppressed.

Slavery systems were under constant attack by the people called Methodist. John Wesley, himself, while preaching in Bristol (the focal point for the British slave trade) would have to flee the pulpit on occasion to escape hostile mobs threatened by his commitment to abolishing slavery. In a letter to the early abolishionist William Wilberforce, his last, written just four days prior to his death, Wesley makes this perceptive observation:

> Unless God has raised you up for this very thing, you will be worn out by the opposition of men and devils. But, "if God be for you, who can be against you?" Are all of them together stronger than God? O "be not weary in well doing!" Go on, in the name of God and in the power of his might, til even American slavery shall vanish away before it.[4]

History proves that Wesley's passion for human rights was some of the first fruit bearing seed leading to emancipation less than 75 years later.

Another example of God gifting the Church against systems that oppress related to child labor where children were exploited with long hours and little pay. This system would fall under the anointed hand of Revival as sweat shops would soon be regulated and monitored far more carefully.

Sexist systems succumbed to women raised up by God to take their rightful place, not only in the workplace, but in the pulpit as well.

Abusive prison and legal systems were forced to yield to reform after reform sparked by Godly Spirit-filled people committed to justice and compassion.

Industrial systems committed only to avarice and greed (sometimes called profit motive) were challenged by a church's even stronger commitment to decent wages and reasonable working conditions.

All of this and more was a result of an eighteenth-century movement of the Spirit where obedience to God impulses was rewarded, gifted and empowered to abolish strongholds.

Perhaps the greatest tragedy within the body of Christ in the last 100 years was the division between personal and social gospel.

Fortunately, spiritual authority over abusive systems did not cease in the eighteenth century. Charles Finney marshalled the saints of the nineteenth-century Holiness movement with the cry, "Repent, believe, and become an abolishionist!" Finney warned Spirit-filled Christians with a holiness theology of liberation that those who did not vote the mind of Jesus on justice issues quenched the Spirit within them. Not surprisingly, Professor Timothy Smith convinces most of us that the so-called Social Gospel grew out of (rather than reacted against) the revivalism of the nineteenth century.

Perhaps the greatest tragedy within the body of Christ in the last 100 years was the division between personal and social gospel. I have friends who are sick of form without power, and I have friends who are sick of power without form. Quite frankly, I am sick of both.

Pentecostalism and humanism flourished during a period in the church's history epitomized by the mentality of the "Monkey Trial," with William Jennings Bryan on one side and Clarence Darrow on the other. Pentecostals (and many Evangelicals) had the power but lacked the vision for confronting abusive systems. Humanists (and many Liberals) had the vision but lacked the power for pulling it off.

One was a ghost and the other was a corpse. The church had best be neither. The church had best be a lively organism at war with the rulers of this present darkness at home and abroad, within and without. For a moment let's talk about the vision for a church that is just such an organism.

A contemporary vision for a church gifted and empowered to overcome sin in persons and systems focuses on Spirit-filled persons, like Stephen in Acts 6-7, who are best equipped to serve. Spirit-filled persons must be profoundly offended by sin at whatever level and on whatever front. Spirit-filled persons must pray, write, vote, march, shore up, knuckle down, dig in and speak out.

> *Spirit-filled persons must pray, write, vote, march, shore up, knuckle down, dig in and speak out.*

Today's Spirit-filled church must attack abusive political systems. Basic human rights are denied around the world. Do I sit back and do nothing while black sisters and brothers in South Africa have no vote and few privileges? Surely the demon apartheid would yield to a Spirit-filled Church.

What about the Palestinians and Israel? What is the price of peace? Holy Spirit-filled Christians must pray for wisdom as to West Bank occupation and an international Jerusalem.

What about India, which voted on equal job opportunities for lower-caste peoples only to capitulate to upper-caste rioting? Can Spirit-filled Christians make a difference or do we continue simply to send an occasional dollar (as important as that may be) to the far-away poor?

What about China's democracy movement where young and old alike are on the brink of total despair? Over 1,500 so-called "political dissidents" were executed last year alone.

What about Thailand where 20% of the Thai women between the ages of 18 and 33 are prostitutes and 80% of those have AIDS?

What about the USA, now in apparent retreat in a war against drugs that could consume so many of our neighbors that the rest of us are forced to bolt our doors?

Does all of this tend to overwhelm? I remind you that the recent reunification movement in Germany began as one church (soon joined by other churches) started to pray one night a week specifically for reform. In less than a year the wall came down. Surely God is concerned about such things. If God is concerned, then God is already at work looking for a church to move into the mainstream of God's already intercession. We must pray for a vision. We must continue to pray until the vision consumes us. Then we must rise up and take the land.

Review

The gifts of the Holy Spirit are supernatural ministries available to the various parts of the body of Christ enabling them to minister effectively within their own spheres of influence. Since our spheres are different, out gifts will be different. Why should an ear want gifts appropriate for the eye? The gifts of the Holy Spirit usually surface within the context of ministry. Gifts usually accompany obedience to a God impulse. Spirit-filled Christians are thoroughly offended by sin in persons and systems. Nothing is too big or too small for God's concern. God is already at work within every sphere sowing that we might reap.

Recently I attended a special session of the General Conference of the Methodist Church in India. Listen to this prayer written by one of the District Superintendents.

May God plague you and torment you,
May God set an impossible task before you and dare
     you to meet it,
May God give you strength to do your best,
And then, but only then, may God grant you God's peace!

Study Questions:

1. What is the difference between a natural "talent" and a gift of the Holy Spirit?
2. How many spiritual gifts are there and why is the number significant?
3. How are the gifts of the Spirit used?
4. How does one receive the gifts?
5. Can you name any of *your* spiritual gifts?

Notes

[1]Wesley's *Works*, Vol. 5, p. 214.

[2]Wesley's *Works*, Vol. 3, p. 305.

[3]Wesley's *Works*, Vol. 3, p. 305.

[4]Wesley's *Works*, Vol. 13, p. 153.

Sanctification was frequently referred to by Wesley as "Entire Sanctification," or "Christian Perfection." Sanctification was usually defined as loving God with all one's heart, mind and strength, and one's neighbor as oneself (Mark 12:33). For Wesley one was entirely sanctified or perfected when love (the fruit) had become pure or devoid of self-interest.

1. The Law is redefined in terms of the moral law—the Law of Christ.
2. Grace fulfills the Law by qualifying, sanctifying, motivating and activating the Spirit-filled Christian.
3. Grace upon grace is not only grace *to be*, but grace *to do*.

CHAPTER

12

We have now come full circle — obedience, disobedience, and back to obedience. In an earlier chapter we defined sanctifying grace as the work of the Holy Spirit

Sanctification: Grace Fulfilling the Law

in process. Here "entire sanctification" or "Christian perfection" defines the *goal*: grace fulfills the law. In order to understand this fully we need to make several necessary connections.

As one might suspect (in light of the fruit of the Spirit), Wesley defined entire sanctification or Christian perfection in terms of love. He writes, "By perfection I mean the humble, gentle, patient love of God, and our neighbour, ruling our tempers, words, and actions."[1] Furthermore (to review the entire doctrine briefly), Wesley believed that one could fall from perfection.

As to the manner, he believed that it was wrought in the soul instantaneously by faith, but that a gradual work both preceded and followed the experience. Although he did not contend for the term "sinless" (a phrase he never used), he did not object to it. Finally, he believed that the experience usually occurred at the time of death, the moment before the soul leaves the body, but that it could (or perhaps should) occur much earlier.

The apostle Paul established the theological precedent for such a doctrine: "Love does no harm to its neighbor. Therefore love is the fulfillment of the law" (Rom. 13:10). In another place, "The entire law is summed up in a single command: "Love your neighbor as yourself" (Gal. 5:14). Since love, as the fruit of the Spirit, has already been established, all we need to do here is remind ourselves that love in the Scriptures has a constant companion — *obedience*: "If you love me, you will obey what I command" (John 14:15); and again, "This is love for God: to obey his commands" (1 John 5:3). This, then, makes the necessary connection between love and perfection, love and obedience, and love (or the fruit of the Spirit/grace) fulfilling the law.

> *Love in the Scriptures has a constant companion —* obedience: "If *you love me, you will obey what I command"* (John 14:15)

Jesus had already set the stage for both Paul and Wesley: "Do not think that I have come to abolish the law of the Prophets; I have not come to abolish them but to fulfill them" (Mt. 5:17). The question now is, how? How does Jesus fulfill the law? In a word, *grace* is the answer. After we have redefined the law in light of our New Testament perspective, we will attempt to speak to this important issue under the following headings: Grace Qualifies, Grace Sanctifies, Grace Motivates, Grace Activates and Grace Upon Grace.

The Law Redefined

Since the law that Jesus fulfills is obviously not the ceremonial or ritual law described in the Torah (the first five books of the Bible), what is the law that Jesus refers to here? Wesley defines law not as the ceremonial or ritual, but as the *moral* law, exemplified by the Ten Commandments and enforced by the prophets. In earlier discussions of the law of sin and death we emphasized the lasting importance of the moral law—a law in perpetuity. Wesley writes,

The moral [law] stands on an entirely different foundation from the ceremonial or ritual law, which was only designed for a temporary restraint upon a disobedient and still-necked people; whereas this [moral law] was from the beginning of the world, being "written not on tables of stone," but on the hearts of all the children of men, when they came out of the hands of the Creator.[2]

The Law of Christ

In the New Testament this moral law is sometimes referred to as the "law of Christ" (1 Cor. 9:21 RSV). The content of the law of Christ is the same as the moral law, but the law of Christ has done away with the condemnation (although not the obedience); the law of Christ has done away with the law as a means of justification and gives us Christian liberty or freedom. Again, I hasten to add, however, that this freedom is not freedom from obedience, but condemnation.

Wesley spent a lifetime fighting antinomianism, "against law," the view that the moral law has no place in the life of believers because believers "are not under law but under grace" (Rom. 6:15). He knew this to be a distortion of Paul's teaching. Once when asked by an antinomian friend to respond to the text from Galatians 4:4-5:

"God sent his Son, . . . to redeem those under law," he writes: "But from what did he redeem them? Not 'from the law'; but 'from guilt, and sin, and hell.' In other words, He redeemed them from the 'condemnation of this law,' not from 'obedience to it.' In this respect they are still, 'not without law to God, but under the law to Christ.'"[3]

In that same place Wesley quickly adds that the freedom here implies that we obey the law of Christ, by free choice, and not by constraint. We keep the commandments of God out of love, not fear.

The Law of the Spirit of Life

In earlier sections we have defined the law of the Spirit of life as the same law as the law of sin and death, but as a result of the new birth the Holy Spirit/grace is at work so that we have both the power and the inclination to obey it. Love, rather than fear, transforms death into life so that the law of God is now "holy, righteous and good" (Rom. 7:12). Wesley writes rather extravagantly,

> The law of God . . . is the fairest offspring of the everlasting Father, the brightest efflux of his essential wisdom, the visible beauty of the Most High. It is the delight and wonder of cherubim and seraphim, and all the company of heaven, and the glory and joy of every wise believer, every well-instructed child of God upon earth.[4]

Little wonder Paul would insist, "Do we, then, nullify the law by this faith? Not at all! Rather, we uphold the law" (Rom. 3:31). Such is the work of grace. Read these verses carefully from 2 Corinthians 3:7-11.

> Now if the ministry that brought death [the law in and of itself], which was engraved in letters on stone, came with glory, . . . will not the ministry of the Spirit [the law of the Spirit of life] be even more glorious? If the ministry that condemns men is glorious, how much more glorious is the ministry that brings righteousness! For what was glorious has no glory now in comparison with the surpassing glory. And if what was fading away came with glory, how much greater is the glory of that which lasts!

As a larger context for this quotation listen to selected passages from just the first four chapters of 2 Corinthians. The law, in and of itself, says "no," grace says "yes," to all of the promises of God (1:18-20). By grace we become "the aroma of Christ among those who are being saved" (2:15). By grace "our competence comes from God; . . . for the letter kills, but the Spirit gives life" (3:5-6). By grace we "are being transformed into his likeness with ever-increasing glory, which comes from the Lord, who is the Spirit" (3:18). Furthermore, "we have this treasure [this grace] in jars of clay to show that this all-surpassing power is from God and not from us. We are hard pressed on every side, but not crushed; perplexed, but not in despair; persecuted, but not abandoned; struck down, but not destroyed" (4:7-9).

By grace, the law, though it is not the way, points to the way. Even more important for us here, by grace the law keeps us in the way. Once again Wesley writes a relevant word,

... yea, allowing we have done with the moral law, as a means of procuring our justification; for we are "justfied freely by his grace, through the redemption that is in Jesus; yet, in another sense, we have not done with this law; For it is still of unspeakable use, First, in convincing us of the sin that yet remains both in our hearts and lives, and thereby keeping us close to Christ, that his blood may cleanse us every moment; Secondly, in deriving strength from our Head into his living members, whereby he empowers them to do what his law commands; and, Thirdly, in confirming our hope of whatsoever it commands and we have not yet attained, — of receiving grace upon grace, till we are in actual possession of the fulness of his promises.[5]

Grace Qualifies

Wesley's sermon "The Wedding Garment" has Matthew 22:12 as its text: "Friend, how did you get in here without wedding clothes?" That verse is taken from the parable of the king who prepared a great wedding banquet for his son and his bride. In this particular culture two invitations were expected — one to ask the guests to attend and the other to announce that the banquet was ready. This king made three invitations, pleading with those invited to attend, but all refused (some mocking, others abusing or even killing some of his messengers).

In this particular culture two invitations were expected — one to ask the guests to attend and the other to announce that the banquet was ready.

After punishing the unworthy guests the king then sent other messengers into the streets to invite anyone who would come to attend. Finally, the banquet hall was filled and each guest had been given a garment enabling them to participate fully in the wedding celebration. When the king realized one of the guests had refused to wear the wedding garment provided, the guest was bound and thrown out into darkness.

The moral to this parable should be fairly obvious. The king is God. The banquet is the Kingdom of heaven. Those invited first were the Jews who refused God's gift of salvation. Those next invited were the Gentiles who accepted and were given the garments of righteousness provided by Jesus Christ and necessary for proper entrance into the celebration. The one refusing the garment represents those who accept the invitation of salvation but who refuse the call to holiness which enables us to enjoy God forever. Ultimately, we cannot accept the invitation of God without accepting God's provision in Jesus Christ — the holiness without which no one shall see God (Heb. 12:14). Wesley puts it this way:

> The righteousness of Christ is doubtless necessary for any soul that enters into glory: But so is personal holiness too, for every child of man. But it is highly needful to be observed, that they are necessary in different respects. The former is necessary to *entitle* us to heaven; the latter to *qualify* us for it. Without the righteousness of Christ we could have no *claim* to glory; without holiness we could have no *fitness* for it. By the former we become members of Christ, children of God, and heirs of the kingdom of heaven. By the latter "we are made meet to be partakers of the inheritance of the saints in light."[6]

Wesley concludes this sermon with this invitation: "Choose life, that ye may live. Choose holiness, by my grace; which is the way, the only way, to everlasting life."[7]

To state all of this a bit differently, grace brings us back full circle to the good news of created in the image of God. We are not only covered by the blood of Jesus Christ so that our sins are forgiven; we are washed by the blood of Jesus Christ so that our sins are removed. The wedding garment, the righteousness of Christ, does not qualify us in the sense that we are pre-Adamic or angelic in our "perfection," but it does qualify us in the sense that we have the mind of Christ so that we love God, ourselves, and others, as Christ loved us. To use still another Wesleyan phrase: When imputed righteousness becomes imparted righteousness we are "ripe for glory."

Grace Sanctifies

In our discussion of the new birth we emphasized that the new birth was the *beginning* of sanctification. If the new birth is the beginning, then entire sanctification or perfection is the *end*. Furthermore, although many within holiness circles identify entire sanctification with the baptism of the Holy Spirit, it has already been established that I believe this to be a mistake. Holy Spirit baptism is the cause, not the effect of sanctification. Holy Spirit baptism is the reason, not a reward for sanctification. We are sanctified as well as justified by grace through faith.

Sanctification as Pure Love

For better than 50 years, whenever Wesley was asked to define Christian perfection, he always referred to various aspects of "pure love": "The loving God with all our heart, mind, soul, and strength. This implies, that no wrong temper, none contrary to love, remains in the soul; and that all the thoughts, words, and actions, are governed by pure love."[8]

That pure love was the work of the Spirit is described in some detail in his well-known sermon: "The Circumcision of the Heart."

Although this sermon was first preached in 1733 (five years before Aldersgate), he later revised the sermon to include all of the classical evangelical doctrines. There Wesley insisted that the only means of establishing the law was by grace through faith. Grace established pardon through faith in the blood of Christ. Grace then grounds us in Jesus Christ, enabling us to proceed swiftly in the way of holiness so that our hearts are circumcised and cleansed from sin. Now we can begin to fulfill the intent of the law — the law of love for God, for self and for neighbor.

If the new birth is the beginning, then entire sanctification or perfection is the end.

Although I have never in my own ministry emphasized a definite second work of grace as isolated from the many other experiences common to the process of sanctification, John Wesley certainly did. I have observed that to isolate a second experience is to lend the impression of having arrived — the "kiss of death" — so that we lose our momentum and start to fall away. Admittedly, Wesley was well aware of the dangers here. He insisted that one should guard against pride by acknowledging that one would grow in grace far more quickly after experiencing perfection than before. Wesley writes,

> God hath now laid "the axe unto the root of the tree, purifying their hearts by faith," and "cleansing all the thoughts of their hearts by the inspiration of his Holy Spirit . . . . " Not that they have already attained all that they shall attain, either are already in this sense perfect. But they daily "go on from strength to strength; beholding" now, "as in a glass, the glory of the Lord, they are changed into the same image, from glory to glory, by the Spirit of the Lord."[9]

Grace Sanctifies by Drawing Rather than Driving

Once while in the Middle East a tour guide was attempting to impress upon a group of tourists how faithfully the sheep in the surrounding fields followed the path of their shepherd. Knowing the sound of the shepherd's voice they would follow single file out across the terrain. Then, while driving through one of the villages, one observant tourist noticed that here was a shepherd apparently driving, not leading, the sheep. Pointing this out to the guide, the guide simply responded: "That's not the shepherd. That's the butcher."

When Wesley was asked how the Methodists should preach perfection, he very wisely said: "Scarce at all those who are not pressing forward: To those who are, always by way of promise; always drawing, rather than driving."[10]

Grace Motivates

The law, in and of itself, tempts us into believing that we can use the law to make some claim upon God. By the same token, legalism attempts to put God under obligation to ourselves. Yet another of the Accuser's lies. Grace, on the other hand, reminds us repeatedly that we are the ones under obligation.

Grace is the prodigal son, aware of his own unworthiness. Legalism is the elder son, jealous of his brother's redemption. Grace is the grateful worker receiving full pay though he was hired in the evening. Legalism is the resentful worker receiving the same pay though he was hired in the morning. Grace is the repentant sinner receiving mercy. Legalism is the self-righteous Pharisee oblivious to mercy. Grace is the woman caught in adultry with no one left to condemn her. Legalism is an angry crowd looking for condemnation. Grace loves its enemy. Legalism loves only its friend. Grace obeys God out of gratitude. Legalism obeys God out of compunction. Grace is justice and mercy. Legalism is justice alone. Grace loves. Legalism fears. Grace responds. Legalism reacts. Grace wants

> *Grace obeys God out of gratitude. Legalism obeys God out of compunction. Grace is justice and mercy. Legalism is justice alone.*

only to please God because God alone is worthy, worthy of praise, worthy of glory, worthy of honor, worthy of our every obedience.

Grace not only empowers; grace motivates. The law of the Spirit of life puts Romans 10:4 — "Christ is the end of the law" — into perspective. Christ is not the end as in "termination" but the end as in "goal" of the law. Grace fixes our eyes on Jesus, "the author and perfecter of our faith, who for the joy set before him endured the cross, scorning its shame, and sat down at the right hand of the throne of God" (Heb. 12:2). The word "joy" in that passage is key. Grace draws. Legalism drives. Grace abhors sin. Legalism fears death and hell.

In his sermon, "The Original, Nature, Property, and Use of the Law," Wesley concludes with these words:

> . . . Abhor sin itself, far more than the punishment of it. Beware of bondage of pride, of desire, of anger; of every evil temper, or word, or work. "Look unto Jesus"; and in order thereto, look more and more into the perfect law, "the law of liberty"; and "continue therein"; so shalt thou daily "grown in grace, and in the knowledge of our Lord Jesus Christ."[11]

Recently a friend wrote to me her "thoughts for the morning" which speak eloquently to grace that motivates.

O Holy Spirit, set me afire!
Take out of me any inclination to view my life as dull,
    routine, uninteresting.
Scrub out of my thoughts any vestige of the opinion that the
    Christian life is one of obligation and restriction.
Set me afire, Lord, I repeat. Heighten in me a blazing desire
    to do your will, to be about your business.
Excite me with the opportunities you have for me. Give me
    the Pauline zeal to serve, to tell others of your activity in
    my life.
Burn away fear of being thought strange. Clarify the one path
    you have designated as mine. Set my foot upon it, my
    face toward Jerusalem, and give me eagerness for the
    journey. Amen.[12]

Amen, indeed!

Grace Activates

Grace is active. Grace is costly. Grace is blood, real blood; sweat, real sweat; and tears, real tears. Grace moves us beyond the pew and into the program, beyond the steeple and into the street, beyond the talk and into the walk. Someone has said: "All other religions say: 'Do!' Christianity says: 'Done!'" That statement packs a lot of truth. Christ has done it all. Faith in him alone puts us right with God, heals the brokenness of our time and makes us fit to share the heritage of God's glory. Faith, however, has its inevitable fruit. We too easily forget that although we are saved by grace through faith, we are judged by our works.

Grace moves us beyond the pew and into the program, beyond the steeple and into the street, beyond the talk and into the walk.

Last year I wrote an article for a denominational magazine where I asked the question, "Can salvation and judgment dwell in the same house?" John Wesley (the man of one book) might well have responded, "Let God speak for himself": "Godly sorrow brings repentance that leads to salvation ... (2 Cor. 7:10); for we must all appear before the judgment of Christ, that each one may receive what is due for the things done while in the body" (2 Cor. 5:10). Connect these thoughts with "The dead were judged according to what they had done ..." (Rev. 20:12); "for by grace you have been saved through faith — and this not from yourselves ..., for we are God's workmanship, created in Christ Jesus to do good works" (Eph. 2:8-10), and the answer, at least from a biblical point of view, seems apparent. Time and again, the Bible affirms that if we are indeed saved by grace through faith, then clearly we are judged by our works, the inevitable fruit of that salvation.

> *Both salvation and judgment are absolutely essential to the integrity of the gospel.*

Simply stated, God acts primarily as creator, savior and judge. As creator, God fashions us in God's own image. As savior, God acts as an immediate result of God's spontaneous love to restore the image that has been lost. As judge, God acts as to whether or not that restored image bears its necessary fruit. As Christians, by virtue of our faith in Christ, the power of the Holy Spirit is released to fulfill all righteousness.

God's judgment against sin makes salvation not only necessary but unattainable unless God intervenes. That is the point, however. Grace is available. We are without excuse. Wesley wrote, "Methodists that do not fulfill all righteousness deserve the hottest place in the lake of fire." Salvation and judgment link faith and works as a peculiar Wesleyan legacy. Judgment, however, is not designed simply to keep the justified honest, but to remind us that ultimately we know a tree by its fruit.

Once again, we are saved by grace through faith and are judged by our works. Grace activates the will and empowers the mind, body, and spirit so that God's love is revealed *to* us in salvation and *through* us in judgment. In a phrase: our actions bear witness to so great a salvation. Both salvation and judgment are absolutely essential to the integrity of the gospel. Salvation nurtures the root; judgment inspects the fruit. Again, grace activates. Grace puts battleships on the open seas, not in mudpuddles. Grace puts locomotives in front of freight cars, not little red wagons. Grace rolls up its sleeves and goes to work as proof of its own salvation. In the Greek, faith is a verb as well as a noun. Faith is both confession and obedience, being and doing, talking and walking. I've always liked this little prayer. It sits on top of my computer even as I write these words:

The fruit of Silence is Prayer
The fruit of Prayer is Faith
The fruit of Faith is Love
The fruit of Love is Service
The fruit of Service is Peace

Mother Teresa

Grace upon Grace

A brief commentary on two final quotations from John Wesley will conclude this chapter on sanctification — grace fulfilling the law. In the first quotation Wesley writes,

There is . . . the closest connexion that can be conceived, between the law and the gospel. On the one hand, the law continually makes way for, and points us to, the gospel; on the other, the gospel continually leads us to a more exact fulfilling of the law. . . . We feel that we are not sufficient for these things; yea, that "with man this is impossible:" But we see a promise of God, . . . it is done unto us according to our faith; and "the righteousness of the law is fulfilled in us," through faith which is in Christ Jesus.[13]

The second quotation has already been cited so I give you just the last few lines: "For it [the law] is still of unspeakable use, . . . in confirming our hope of whatever it commands and we have not yet attained, — of receiving grace upon grace, "till we are in actual possession of the fullness of His promises."[14]

These two passages yield two key phrases. The first insists that "with man this [fulfilling the law] is impossible." According to Wesley, prevenient grace draws and enables us to respond to God through faith in Jesus Christ, God's provision for our salvation. At that point, however, grace has not completed its work. Salvation, the whole of it, is grace upon grace. We are wooed by grace. We are saved by grace. We are sanctified by grace. With God (by grace through faith) all things are possible indeed.

The second passage speaks specifically of "receiving grace upon grace, 'till we are in actual possession of the fullness of His promises.'" Again, this is not only grace *to be*, but grace *to do*.

I close with a principle already alluded to that could well change your life. Agree with God now to take from you some area of resistance to God's best, a sin or a problem in a relationship not yet yielded to God. Note, I'm not asking to you to give this problem to God. If you could give it to God out of your own strength, you

> *Your willingness to let God work releases the power of grace/Spirit*

would not need God. I am simply asking you to allow God's Holy Spirit to take it from you as you renew your faith and trust in Jesus Christ.

Here is the principle. Your willingness to let God work releases the power of grace/Spirit so that the next time you are tempted with this particular temptation your first inclination will be to resist it. Grace says it will be easier to yield to God than to temptation. Then at that moment you renew your faith and trust once again to prepare for the next trial and so ultimately fulfill the law. Test this principle. It works. Grace upon grace can and will fulfill the law.

> Closer and closer let us cleave
>> To His beloved embrace;
> Expect His fullness to receive,
>> And grace to answer grace.

Charles Wesley

Review

Although grace does not fulfill the ceremonial or ritual law, grace does fulfill the moral law, the law of Christ. Christ is not the end of the law in the sense of termination but the end of the law in the sense of goal. He is the goal of grace through faith. We are to love as he loved. We are to minister as he ministered. We are to resist sin as he resisted sin. Do not despair! What is impossible with us is possible with God. Grace upon grace completes the circle so that good news that yields to bad news now yields to good news. Entire sanctification has us "ripe for glory."

> O Christ, my life, possess me utterly.
> Take me and make a little Christ of me.
> If I am anything but thy Father's son,
> 'Tis something not yet from the darkness won.
> Oh, give me light to live with open eyes.
> Oh, give me life to hope above all skies.
> Give me thy Spirit to haunt the Father with my cries.

From *Diary of an Old Soul* by George MacDonald

If you have to read those lines several times to get the full significance, it is well worth the effort. "Oh, that we might know the Lord! Let us press on to know him, and he will respond to us as surely as the coming of dawn or the rain of early spring" (Hos. 6:3, *The Living Bible*).

Study Questions:

1. What is the law of Christ?
2. How does grace fulfill the law?
3. How does grace qualify or sanctify us for heaven?
4. How does grace motivate and activate?
5. What is the significance of "grace upon grace?"

Notes

[1]Wesley's *Works*, Vol. 11, p. 446.

[2]Wesley's *Works*, Vol. 10, p. 281.

[3]Wesley's *Works*, Vol. 10, p. 281.

[4]Wesley's *Works*, Vol. 5, pp. 438f.

[5]Wesley's *Works*, Vol. 5, p. 444.

[6]Wesley's *Works*, Vol. 7, p. 314.

[7]Wesley's *Works*, Vol. 7, p. 317.

[8]Wesley's *Works*, Vol. 11, p. 394.

[9]Wesley's *Works*, Vol. 11, p. 378f.

[10]Wesley's *Works*, Vol. 11, p. 387.

[11]Wesley's *Works*, Vol. 5, p. 446.

[12]"Thoughts" in a personal letter from Fern M. Underwood.

[13]Wesley's *Works*, Vol. 5, pp. 313f.

[14]Wesley's *Works*, Vol. 5, p. 444.

Matthew 15:8-9   *1 Corinthians 10:13*
Acts 15:7-11   *Galatians 3:3-5, 10*
Romans 7:12, 16-18 *Ephesians 1:7-10, 13-14*

A new legalism leads to condemnation or guilt that is supposed or neurotic—what I sometimes refer to as a "ditch to ditch" theology.

---

1. Law can be revelatory or legalistic.

2. The old legalism, which plagued Paul and the apostles, has taken on more subtle forms emerging as a new legalism.

3. Grace gets us free and keeps us free from legalism, both old and new, as it reestablishes the true character of the law.

CHAPTER
13

This last chapter will serve as a postscript and review. Many of us tend to learn most easily at the point of someone else's need, not our own. We read something and find ourselves thinking, "I wish old 'whats-his-foot' would read this. She really needs that." Similarly, we usually do not learn at the point of our bias. That simply reinforces what we know already. We must learn at the point of our need.

Against a New Legalism: The Roads Back into the Law Are Legion

This book is for you. It was not written for someone who will never read it. If you are an evangelical, perhaps you need to learn at the point of a broader world view where grace speaks to systems as well as to individuals. If you are committed to the social gospel, perhaps you need to learn at the point of the power available through personal faith in Jesus Christ for abolishing strongholds in persons and systems.

The point is there is something here for all of us if we will open our hearts and minds to what the Spirit is doing. Time taken to read these pages could be used for doing something else. We might as well make it count for good. Ask the question: "What would God teach me today?"

The ministry of the apostle Paul is an interesting story. Converted in Damascus around 35 A.D. following an encounter with Jesus just outside the city, a blinding vision informed him of a mission among Gentiles as well as Jews. Paul spent the next three years in the Arabian desert, no doubt sorting out his new-found faith. When he returned to Damascus some of the Jews there conspired to kill him. He narrowly escaped through a window in the city wall and was taken by Barnabas to Jerusalem to meet the apostles. All but James and Peter refused to see him since he had not yet overcome his rather considerable reputation as a persecutor of Christians. He preached boldly throughout Jerusalem, but within two weeks he was once again threatened by Jews. He was sent immediately to Caesarea and then home to Tarsus.

> *Paul spent the next three years in the Arabian desert, no doubt sorting out his new-found faith.*

Eventually, Barnabas brought Paul to Antioch, where together they ministered to Jews but also to Greeks (or Gentiles), for the first time calling themselves Christians. That created a problem. Can Christians become Christians without first becoming Jews and submitting to all of the Jewish laws and customs? Before working through the solution to this problem, let me give you just a bit more history.

While Paul was in Tarsus and then in Antioch, God had been preparing Peter (a bit of a purist) for Paul's important ministry to Gentiles as well as to Jews. First of all, Peter and John had seen the Holy Spirit poured out on the Samaritans (Acts 8:14-17), just as the Holy Spirit had been poured out on the Jews at Pentecost. The significance of this was in the hostile relationship between Jews and the Samaritans. The Samaritans were decendants of Jews who had broken solidarity with the Jews during the Babylonian exile (586 BC) by remaining behind, intermarrying with their captors and eventually forgetting Hebrew. When the Jewish exiles returned to Jerusalem to rebuild the Temple these "half-breeds" offered assistance but were summarily rejected as non-Jews and sent back to Samaria. There they built a rival temple on Mt. Gerizim. Tragically, for the

500 or so years prior to the birth of Jesus, Jews and Samaritans had been going back and forth between each other's temples desecrating them with dead men's bones. In a phrase, they hated each other.

Soon after Peter and John had seen the Holy Spirit poured out on the Samaritans, Peter journeyed to Joppa where he stayed in the home of Simon the tanner. Since tanners worked with the skins of animals it was unkosher for Peter the Jew even to associate with Simon, let alone stay with him. Next we read of the vision of unclean animals (which God pronounced clean) being lowered in a sheet and the visit from the servants of Cornelius inviting Peter to Caesarea. In Caesarea we see not half-breeds but full blown pagans (Gentiles, like most of us) receiving the Holy Spirit just as the Jews did at Pentecost.

Peter had apparently learned his lesson, at least to a degree. Soon afterwards we find him in Antioch with Paul observing a ministry among the Gentiles. Unfortunately, the visit ended awkwardly when after a few days Paul criticized Peter (twice) for backing away from Gentiles when Jews from Jerusalem arrived in Antioch and began to complain about Peter's association with pagans. Peter returned to Jerusalem and Paul and Barnabas set out on their first missionary journey.

Now, the problem addressed in this last chapter (and indeed in the book as a whole) comes into sharper focus. Everywhere that Paul and Barnabas went the gospel of Jesus Christ freed people from the bondage of sin. Tragically "judaizers," would then come in behind them and attempt to place those just released back under a bondage to the law by insisting

Everywhere that Paul and Barnabas went the gospel of Jesus Christ freed people from the bondage of sin.

that Gentile Christians be circumcised and obey the law of Moses (including the ritual and ceremonial law) as well. Repeatedly Paul would free them up. Repeatedly someone else would put them back into bondage. These Judaizers not only attempted to add an unnecessary burden to Paul's message of grace, they pursued and persecuted Paul throughout the province of Asia (2 Cor. 1:8ff.). Understandably at the conclusion of this journey Paul went to Jerusalem to sort these matters out. The solution is significant indeed.

When Paul reached Jerusalem the apostles called a council. Both sides were heard and (fortunately for us) a decision was reached to add *nothing* to Paul's gospel. Even Titus (a Gentile traveling with Paul) was not circumcised (although I am certain that he had a few anxious moments). Paul was given complete freedom to preach and teach without the burden of the entire law being added. Peter concluded,

> Brothers, you know that some time ago God made a choice among you that the Gentiles might hear from my lips the message of the gospel and believe. God, who knows the heart, showed that he accepted them by giving the Holy Spirit to them, just as he did to us. He made no distinction between us and them, for he purified their hearts by faith. Now then, why do you try to test God by putting on the necks of the disciples a yoke that neither we nor our fathers have been able to bear? No! We believe it is through *the grace of our Lord Jesus* that we are saved, just as they are (Acts 15:7-11, italics mine).

Just as the Judaizers attempted to add to the gospel an unnecessary burden, today Christians, perhaps unintentionally, do the same.

Only these stipulations were then given: the Gentiles should not eat meat from strangled animals leaving the blood still in them (since blood is the sign of life); they should not eat food that had been dedicated to idols; they should not be immoral (as Gentiles were prone to be); and they should remember the poor (which thing they were most eager to do, Gal. 2:10). Paul left Jerusalem with a letter for Gentile Christians that secured their new-found freedom. So, how does this relate to a "new legalism?"

Just as the Judaizers attempted to add to the gospel an unnecessary burden, today Christians, perhaps unintentionally, do the same. Some of these attempts are blatantly obvious. Some are more devious and subtle. After briefly working through the biblical precedents for dealing with an old legalism, we will address our own topic,

"Against a New Legalism," under these headings: A New Legalism Defined; Getting Free; Staying Free; and Grace Re-establishing the True Character of the Law.

The Old Legalism

When looking for a biblical precedent for dealing with an old legalism we are at an immediate disadvantage. The Greek language used by the New Testament writers had no word group to denote "legalism."[1] They had no ready-made terms to locate the problem. So, first of all, we must identify the concept.

Paul seems to have at least two references for "law" — one revealed by the Creator (revelatory) and the other imposed by creation (legalistic). Obviously, Romans 7:12 — "The law is holy, and the commandment is holy, righteous and good" — is the revelatory usage. On the other hand, Galatians 3:10 — "All who rely on observing [or rely on "the works of"] the law are under a curse" — would be the legalistic.

> *Legalism grieves where God would not have us grieve.*

In other places we have already established that the law is good — revelatory. We have also established that there is a Jewish *mis*interpretation of the law that is bad — legalistic. Revelatory "reveals" the mind of God and drives us to grace by virtue of our inability to obey the law. Legalism seeks by means of obeying the law (however inadequately) to *earn* favor with God. Important for Paul, therefore, in identifying law as legalistic is the phrase "the works of the law." The end of our own effort alone is always death. No amount of energy is wasted in trying to avoid the subtle temptation of thinking that we can somehow "measure up." No amount of energy is wasted in embracing the grace of God revealed through faith in Jesus Christ.

Legalism grieves where God would not have us grieve. I sometimes require my students to struggle with identifying the least you can believe and still be a Christian. What is the lowest common denominator? The reason? If the *least* you can believe is sufficient to put you in right relationship with God, then the least you can believe is the *most* you can require of others lest we require more of people than God would require. That was a problem in Paul's day. That is still a problem in our own day.

A New Legalism Defined

From the outset our primary text has been Romans 8:1-2. The phrase "no condemnation" spoken of in that text is key. Legalism breeds condemnation or guilt that is both real and supposed. A new legalism leads to condemnation or guilt that is supposed or neurotic — what I sometimes refer to as a "ditch to ditch" theology. Real guilt involves only what we are *in God's sight*, no more, no less — we are measured by God's standard. Neurotic guilt tacks on a human standard — we are measured by the standards of those around us. Compare neurotic guilt with grace, and the contrast is even more apparent. Grace seeks the mind of Christ. Neurotic guilt seeks the approval of one's peers. Let me illustrate.

I frequently remind young people that most of them do what they do, say what they say, even wear what they wear because of their peers. Furthermore, the polls tell us that 90 percent of the major decisions in life are set in concrete by the age of 22. That means that if you are a 17 year-old and like most who are 17, you will make 90 percent of the major decisions in your life within the next five years.

> *Ninety percent of the major decisions in life are set in concrete by the age of 22.*

Even more frightening, if you do not resist peer pressure at 17, you probably will not resist peer pressure at 22. By that time you will have allowed your well-meaning peers to influence your future more than God. The real tragedy is that although God has far more invested in that future than those around you, you have looked somewhere else for the answers to life's most important questions. Again, grace seeks the mind of Christ. A new legalism "keeps up with the Joneses" — the breeding ground for condemnation and neurotic guilt.

A new legalism gets even more subtle than that. It gets "spiritual." Just as an old legalism held to the "works of the law" as the means of justification, a new legalism holds to certain characteristics of spirituality as the means of sanctification. Again, Paul states the problem succinctly,

> Are you so foolish? After beginning with the Spirit, are you now trying to obtain your goal by human effort? Have you suffered so much for nothing — if it really was for nothing? Does God give you his Spirit and work miracles among you because you observe the law, or because you believe what you heard? (Gal. 3:3-5).

The "law" in this passage is, for the most part, ceremonial. Have we today invented a new ceremonial law, a new legalism? Perhaps.

Clearly sanctification, like justification, is the work of the Spirit. The whole of salvation is by grace through faith. A new legalism, however, would ask, "Do you have faith enough? Is your faith really strong enough to save you, let alone sanctify you?" Alas, a new legalism forever misses the point! It is Jesus Christ who saves *and* sanctifies, not *our* feelings or actions, and he is strong enough to save and sanctify anyone no matter how weak their faith might be. Once again, we are not saved or sanctified by feelings or works but according to the grace revealed in God's promise to forgive those who place their faith and trust in Jesus Christ.

All of this means that one should never make the mistake of comparing one person's spirituality with another's. Since no two people have the same point of departure, no one person can be typed as more or less spiritual than someone else. A new legalism implies that becoming a Christian makes me better than someone else. Grace insists that becoming a Christian makes me better than what *I* was. The subtlety here can get even more complicated.

Faith itself can become a new legalism. God is not subject to cause and effect, at least as we understand it. In some circles well-meaning Christians believe that God is bound to deliver according to our faith — whatever I ask for believing "in the name of Jesus" (almost as if that were some sort of magical formula), God is obligated to give. I sometimes refer to such a doctrine as "confess it; possess it," or "name it; claim it," or "blab it; grab it." In effect, our faith becomes a work, a new legalism.

To be sure, faith has its own effect, but faith as the cause is itself a gift from God. We do not love God in order to get from God. That is not the meaning of *agape* love, the fruit of the Spirit which gives expecting nothing in return. We love God for one reason and one reason only: God is worthy of love. We love God for who God is; *then* the effects will follow.

Another new legalism involves the gifts of the Spirit. I am sometimes asked if Christians should seek certain spiritual gifts. I usually say, "no." The reason is that the moment I seek one particular gift of the Spirit and receive it, almost inevitably I find myself thinking: "Thank God I finally got spiritual enough to receive this gift." A new legalism whispers that I must, therefore, be more spiritual than those who do not have this gift. Grace, on the other hand, reminds us that the gifts are just that — gifts, not wages. The gifts are given to enable me to minister more effectively within my own sphere of influence, not someone else's. A new legalism wants you to have *my* gifts. Grace wants you to have *your* gifts. A new legalism covets your gifts. Grace is content with its own gifts. A new legalism associates gifts with spirituality. Grace associates gifts with God's matchless generosity.

> *We love God for one reason and one reason only: God is worthy of love.*

A new legalism associates spirituality with *doing* rather than *being*. Admittedly, faith acts (make no mistake about that), but faith creates action, action does not create faith. I act because I am spiritual. I am not spiritual because I act. So, why is this so important? Are we not playing with words? No! There is a great deal at stake here. True spirituality as the creation of faith, rather than works, does several significant things. It eliminates human pride; it exalts God (not people); it makes salvation available to everyone; it admits that we cannot keep the law (even the moral law) on our own — we need help; and it establishes one's spirituality on a basis of relationship (not performance).

Before moving on to a new heading, one last form of a new legalism (though their name is Legion) needs to be discussed: it is experiential. We have already mentioned that although your "crisis" experience may have been wonderful, no one experience can be made normative for the Church. There is an old story of a town drunk stumbling out of a tavern late at night, crossing a field and falling into an open well. Just as he is about to drown he prays, "God, save me and I am yours." At that moment someone miraculously appears and pulls him out. Talk about crisis. For the rest of his life the redeemed drunk takes people to the same tavern, gets them drunk on the same beer, leads them out across the same field, pushes them into the same well and waits for them to pray the same prayer before pulling them out. He no doubt lost far more than he saved.

Once again the old legalism (or works of the law) implies that we *earn* our reward or punishment according to the standard of our performance. A new legalism implies that God loves us to the degree that we obey God. In other words, if I do a whole lot of good things, God will love me a whole lot. If I do not do quite so many good things, then God will not love me quite so much — I must get good to get God! Grace, on the other hand, says that you cannot do enough bad things to make God love you any less and you cannot do enough good things to make God love you any more — God already loves you to the maximum!

Legalism, old or new, cannot take its eyes off sin (the Pharisees rejoiced whenever they discovered a new sin). Grace keeps its eyes on Jesus; grace roots out sin and has ample power to overcome it. Legalism reveals sin but is powerless to overcome it. Grace is life. Legalism is death. Grace is relationship. Legalism is separation. Grace is deliverance. Legalism is punishment. Grace heals. Legalism complains because Jesus worked the miracle on the Sabbath. Grace anoints the feet of Jesus. Legalism condemns the woman for the sins of her past. Grace convicts and leads to repentance, faith and forgiveness. Legalism haranges and leads to frustration, doubt and condemnation. Grace accepts freedom from Christ. Legalism demands freedom from systems. Grace gives liberally. Le-

> *Grace . . . says that you cannot do enough bad things to make God love you any less and you cannot do enough good things to make God love you any more — God already loves you to the maximum!*

galism gives 10%. Grace is the spirit of the law — the law of the Spirit of life. Legalism (old and new) is the letter of the law — a law of sin and death.

Getting Free

Now that we have established the problem, we must now address the solution. How can we avoid a new legalism and at the same time continue to grow in grace? John Wesley, you remember, sought to avoid the roads back into "the works of the law" — legalism — by defining sanctification in terms of pure or perfect love, not specific actions. In other words, grace is an emotion (God given love) ruling our actions. Legalism is an action (works-righteousness) ruling our emotions.

Jesus spoke about condemnation or acquittal coming from the heart. Addressing the Pharisees he quotes Isaiah: "These people say they honor me, but their hearts are far away. Their worship is worthless, for they teach their man-made laws instead of those from God" (Mt. 15:8-9, *The Living Bible*). Jesus spoke against such legalism for good reason. He too was plagued with frail flesh and must have been tempted to add an agenda of his own. So how did he manage to overcome temptation at every turn? Surely he holds the key.

> *We theologians watch the early church apologists fight fiercely against the Gnostics for the first 300 years of church history for good reason.*

Although Jesus Christ was the Son of the living God, a fully divine participant in the Godhead, he was also fully human. Make no mistake about that. Although none of us fully understands it (heresy is born when little minds attempt to solve big paradoxes), Jesus was fully God and fully human. We theologians watch the early church apologists fight fiercely against the Gnostics for the first 300 years of church history for good reason. They denied the humanity of Christ. They tried to give us a Jesus with his feet off the ground so that we have no blood, no sacrifice, no redemption, no atonement and no reconciliation with

God. Jesus was fully human and in becoming human he divested himself, not of his deity, but of the attributes of deity, including an inherent divine power (Phil. 2:6-7). So, how did he avoid sin and work miracles? By the power of the Holy Spirit — grace.

I sometimes refer to myself as a charismatic. Perhaps you have suspected as much. All I mean by that, however, is that I firmly believe that the same power of the Holy Spirit available to Jesus is available to us today so that the things that he did, we can do. In fact, as a church, the body of Jesus Christ, we can do even "greater things than these" (Jn. 14:12). Notice that definition makes no reference to specific gifts or styles of worship. It simply affirms that if Jesus had to rely upon the power of the Holy Spirit, how much more must we rely upon the power of the Holy Spirit and make ourselves available to all that God offers through faith in Christ. If you feel overcome with temptation and sin, do not despair.

> No temptation has seized you except what is common to man. And God is faithful; he will not let you be tempted beyond what you can bear. But when you are tempted, he will also provide a way out so that you can stand up under it (1 Cor. 10:13).

Legalism breeds despair. Grace, the power of the Holy Spirit, breeds hope. Since Christ yielded perfectly to grace, he could provide a sinless sacrifice for all of our sins. As a result of that perfect obedience God has sent us the Holy Spirit, available to us by a simple act of faith, so that we can now be free. We can now choose our own master. Paul writes,

> Don't you realize that you can choose your own master. You can choose sin (with death) or else obedience (with acquittal). The one to whom you offer yourself — he will take you and be your master and you will be his slave. Thank God that though you once chose to be slaves of sin, now you have obeyed with all your heart the teaching to which God has committed you. And now you are free from your old master, sin; and you have become slaves to your new master, righteousness (Rom. 7:16-18, *The Living Bible*).

Again, do not despair. The grace of God redirects our attention.

Although the law (as revelation) hates sin, grace loves obedience. Guilt cannot produce righteousness but the power of the Holy Spirit can. The law is like a sign posted at the waters' edge: "No Swimming, Sharks!" Although your swim might be ruined you are not angry with those who put up the sign. Nevertheless, the sign does not get rid of the sharks. Grace does (or at least closes their mouths to human flesh). The hymn writers tell us, "Trust and Obey." Trust releases the power to obey. Faith in Jesus Christ sets us free from the law of sin and death — legalism. Getting free, however, is one thing, but staying free is another.

Staying Free

The subtlety of a new legalism is even more dangerous for those who are wanting to stay free than for those who are wanting to get free. It seems that everyone has a formula.

I am always hesitant to describe my own spiritual "walk with God." What works for me might not necessarily work for someone else. For example, for an extended period of my life, although I belonged to a church, I had no church home where I felt that I could honestly bare my soul and seek counsel from those who would pray for me daily. The only way that I felt that I could survive was to spend two to three hours a day, seven days a week, in the Word of God. I got to the place where I could probably give you off the top of my head a summary of what was in every chapter of the Bible, Genesis to Revelation. When pressed to share that, however, those listening frequently felt as if that was the answer to their own spirituality — a new legalism. As important as time in the Word of God is, that much time might be bondage for one and freedom for another.

Styles of Spirituality that Bind

I recently met a young man who felt that it was important for him to spend a certain amount of time intentionally before God each morning. That was priority and nothing could change it. After watching the man for some time, I began to realize that such a noble commitment was beginning to undermine his integrity in other areas of his life.

He missed a breakfast appointment because he had not finished his "devotions." He reneged on promises knowing that his promise to God came first. Before long his fiancee began to resent his dogged spirit. Eventually, she cancelled their wedding plans. Even his friends began to shy away from such inflexible intolerance. My advice was to "lighten up," and "chill out." Time alone with God is important, but spirituality as another form of legalism quickly reaches a point of diminishing returns. He is still trying to recover.

Balance and Passion

One cure for legalism could be balance. Balance does not dispense with passion, however. I have heard it said that fanatics go crazy over the letter of the law whereas radicals go crazy over the spirit of the law. No one respects a fanatic but radical, well that is a different matter. This world will not yield to half-way measures. The church that I am a part of could use a few Spirit-filled radicals. The Spirit-filled radical is motivated by the love of God and neighbor. Again, emotion rules action. The legalist fanatic is motivated by cause and effect. Action rules emotion. Admittedly, this is an oversimplification but the point is still valid. Keeping free from the bondage of legalism requires flexibility and balance but not without passion.

Obedience Goals and Faithfulness Goals

Let me give you a few principles — faithfulness goals, not obedience goals. Obedience goals establish the kinds of "numbers" that easily succumb to a new legalism inviting defeat. Faithfulness goals establish principles and the numbers take care of themselves. Let me illustrate.

An obedience goal attempts to spend an hour a day with God. If we only spend 50 minutes, then we have failed — bondage. A faithfulness goal seeks a closer walk with God and then establishes the kinds of principles consistent with such a goal. For example, God is near and I want to acknowledge God in all things. God and I will still have the hour together, probably more, but without the legalistic time frame — freedom.

I just went jogging with a prominent businessman who is convinced that if the business world would refuse to sell out to the profit motive as its only priority (an obedience goal), and commit itself to better products and services (a faithfulness goal), then the profits would eventually take care of themselves. Some want their churches run on business principles. I want businesses run on biblical principles.

One faithfulness goal that tends to keep me free from a new legalism simply determines to submit to one other significant person on a weekly basis. During our time together that person does not set the agenda; I set the agenda. I have already reviewed my journal for the week so that I am aware of the cutting edge; what God is presently teaching me. Then my friend loves me enough to hold me accountable in the areas of my life where I need to be growing. He also prays for me daily by name. This form of "discipling" works for me. It might work for you.

Another faithfulness goal that keeps me free from a new legalism but keeps me growing in grace relates (interestingly enough) to service. We have already mentioned the importance of developing an awareness of God's presence in our midst as the heart of spirituality and worship. I find that when I am most aware of God I am usually led to humble service.

> *I find that when I am most aware of God I am usually led to humble service.*

Again, it may be difficult to sin with God looking at you, but it is equally difficult to sit and do nothing. Whenever I acknowledge God in a given situation, I am almost always aware of an opportunity for ministry. I am forever praying that God will make me sensitive to where God is already at work within my own sphere of influence so that I can move into the mainstream of God's already intercession.

Some months ago as I was walking through the metal detector at an airport security station I noticed that the woman sitting behind the monitor X-raying baggage was upset. I could see tears in her eyes. I remember asking God what I could do in less than 30 seconds. In that instant I could see my own briefcase on the screen. Someone had just given me a Communion chalice and there it was clearly outlined inside the briefcase. Standing behind her I asked her if she had any idea what that was. She sniffled and made two or three pretty good guesses.

"No," I said, "that is a Communion chalice which holds the wine or the juice representing the shed blood of Jesus which means that God loves you very, very much."

She immediately spun around on her swivel chair, grabbed my hand and blurted out: "God sent you to me!"

I replied simply, "Yes" (if I had disappeared at that point she would probably have passed out), and walked on to my plane thanking God for yet another opportunity to grow in grace.

Grace Re-establishes the True Character of the Law

What a place to conclude. Grace is so many wonderful things. Just in the last few paragraphs it is freedom; it is passion; it is balance; it is aware of God which sensitizes us to our opportunities for ministry. Perhaps the first principle of law and grace is that although grace does do away with legalism (both old and "new"), grace does not do away with the law (at least as moral or revelatory). Martin Luther described law as the needle that draws the thread of grace. In fact, grace baptizes the law of sin and death and re-establishes its true character as the law of the Spirit of life.

I remember the words of John Calvin: "For the law is in itself bright, but it is only when Christ appears to us in it, that we enjoy its splendour."[2] That is a good word but God forbid that we should give John Calvin the last word. How about this statement from John Wesley?

> . . . it should be particularly observed, that "where sin abounded, grace does much more abound." For not as the condemnation, so is the free gift; but we may gain infinitely more than we have lost . . . . If Adam had not sinned, the Son of God had not died: Consequently that amazing instance of the love of God to man had never existed, which has, in all ages, excited the highest joy, and love, and gratitude from his children. We might have loved God the Creator, God the Preserver, God the Governor; but there would have been no place for love to God the redeemer . . . . We could not then have praised him that, thinking it no robbery to be equal with God, yet emptied himself, took upon him the form of a servant, and was obedient to death, even the death of the cross! This is now

the noblest theme of all the children of God on earth; yea, we need not scruple to affirm, even of angels, and archangels, and all the company of heaven.

> "Hallelujah," they cry,
> "To the King of the sky,
> To the great everlasting I AM;
> To the Lamb that was slain,
> And liveth again,
> Hallelujah to God and the Lamb!"[3]

In the final analysis I do not want John Wesley to have the last word either — not that he could not say it better than I. It is just that John Wesley might have learned from some of our principles as well (John Calvin certainly could have). Perhaps most appropriately we give the last word to the Word of God itself. Time and experience have certainly proven it worthy.

> In him we have redemption through his blood, the forgiveness of sins, in accordance with the riches of God's grace that he lavished on us with all wisdom and understanding. And he made known to us the mystery of his will according to his good pleasure, which he purposed in Christ, to be put into effect when the times will have reached their fulfillment — to bring all things in heaven and on earth together under one head, even Christ . . . .
>
> Having believed, you were marked in him with a seal, the promised Holy Spirit, who is a deposit guaranteeing our inheritance until the redemption of those who are God's own possession . . . (Eph. 1:7-10, 13-14).

Sanctity without starch, indeed!

Study Questions:

1. What is the difference between an old legalism and a new legalism?
2. How does one get free of a new legalism?
3. How does one stay free of a new legalism?
4. How does grace re-establish the true character of the law?

5. Can you identify areas of legalism (old or new) in your own life? If so, what do you intend to do about them?

Notes

[1]Cf. articles by C.E.B. Cranfield, "St. Paul and the Law," *Scottish Journal of Theology*, Vol. 17, 1 (March, 1964), pp. 55ff.; and Daniel P. Fuller, "Paul and the Works of the Law," *Westminster Theological Journal*, Vol. 38, 1 (Fall, 1975), pp. 28ff.

[2]John Calvin, *Commentary on the Epistles of Paul the Apostle to the Corinthians*, Vol. II (trans. by J. Pringle, reprinted Grand Rapids, 1948), p. 183.

[3]Wesley's *Works*, Vol. 6, p. 224.

Made in the USA
Lexington, KY
17 September 2016